Thirty-Six Years
in the White House

Thos F. Pendel—

Thirty-Six Years in the White House

Lincoln—Roosevelt

❦

Thomas F. Pendel

Door-Keeper

APPLEWOOD BOOKS
Bedford, Massachusetts

Thirty-Six Years in the White House
was originally published in 1902.

Thank you for purchasing an Applewood Book.
Applewood reprints America's lively classics—books from
the past that are still of interest to modern readers.
For a free copy of our current catalog, write to:

Applewood Books
P.O. Box 365
Bedford, MA 01730
www.awb.com

ISBN 978-1-55709-923-5

MANUFACTURED IN THE U.S.A.

PREFACE

I am greatly indebted to my friend, Mrs. Rosalie O. Goulding, for valuable assistance in the preparation of this book. Her experience as a journalist has enabled her to advise me in many matters, and acting on her advice, I have endeavored in my Recollections to relate only such events as appear to be worthy of preservation.

THOMAS F. PENDEL.

TO MR. THOMAS F. PENDEL OF THE WHITE HOUSE

The sacred task of personal care,
As portal sentry, standing there,
Protecting him who bore the weight
Of flashing Mars, and Chief of State.

True, swordless sentry watching all,
As brave as love, a living wall,
To trust, protect from foe, or spy—
For that, in ecstasy, would die.

No slumber in the hours of dread,
Who watched each step and breath in bed
When midnight second's solemn gloom
Was brooding danger, certain doom.

Through peaceful public's fatal call,
Great Lincoln fell from villain's ball,
While sentry guarded martyr's chair,
And ever since remaining there.

J. H. BEIDLER.

CONTENTS

ILLUSTRATIONS

Thirty-Six Years in the White House

CHAPTER I

UNDER PRESIDENT LINCOLN

I was born on Analostan Island, near Aqua duct Bridge, at Georgetown, D. C., May 29, 1824. Grandfather Thomas Pendel came from Ireland prior to the Revolutionary War. My maternal grandparents were from Pennsylvania, of old Dutch stock. Grandfather Pendel was in business in Alexandria in the Hudson Bay Fur Company, and accumulated $100,-000, which he spent in aiding the Revolutionary cause, in which he took an active part. His remains lie in the churchyard of Christ Church, Alexandria, where General Washington used to worship.

Father Thomas Pendel was in the Indian Wars, previous to the War of 1812, and also took part in this war. He was an artilleryman, and at the call for volunteers on Lake Erie, reported for duty on an American brig to fight an English frigate. He was in the battle of Black Rock, which site is now the city of Buffalo, and lost an arm by a passing ball from the British. For this he received a pension of ninety dollars a year.

I enlisted in the Marine Corps on March 5, 1846, at Philadelphia; and on February 5, 1847, sailed from Boston on the battleship *Ohio*, bound for Vera Cruz.

In 1861, or 1862, the Metropolitan Police was established by Congress at the Capital, and I made application for and received an appointment on the force. I made the first arrest, with the assistance of "Buck" Essex. The case was that of a fellow named Grady, one of the English Hill toughs. A roundsman said to us, "Boys, you take a walk down Seventh Street, and if you see anything going on, take a hand in it." Just as we got opposite the Patent Office, this Grady had assaulted, or rather was assaulting, a young fellow with a whip. I went up and grabbed him and put him under arrest, then took him to Squire Dunn's court and preferred charges against him. The Squire was busy writing for some time. When he got through he handed me the paper he was writing, and I was so green at the business I did not know what it was, so said: "What is this, Squire?" He replied, "Why, that is the paper of commitment for this fellow. Take him to jail."

On November 3, 1864, Sergeant John Cronin, Alfonso Dunn, Andrew Smith, and myself were ordered to report at the First Precinct, in the old City Hall, at one o'clock in the afternoon. We supposed we were to be detailed for detective work in New York City on account of the great riot then on there, especially as we were ordered to report in citizens' clothes, to conceal our revolvers, and to be sure to have them all clean and in good order. We arrived at the City Hall, and then were told where we were to go, which was to the President's Mansion, there to report to Marshal Lanham, at that time United States Marshal of the District of Columbia, and a bosom friend of Abraham Lincoln.

These were days that tried men's hearts, and women's, too. Men were falling at the front by hundreds, both in the Union and in the Confederate armies. There was weeping and mourning all over the land. Our nation was trembling with anxiety; we were all hoping that the great strife was over or soon to be.

Marshal Lanham took us upstairs and into the President's office, where we were introduced to him and to his two secretaries, Mr. Nicolay and Mr. Hay, the latter now being Secretary of State. We were then instructed to keep a sharp lookout in the different parts of the house, more particularly in the East Room and at the door of the President's office. After we had been on duty about three days, Sergeant John Cronin came to me and said, "Pendel, I want you to take my place near the President's office, and I will send your dinner to you." I took his place, and he sent my dinner up to me, but I think that was the last duty on the force he ever performed. He had other business in the city.

On the first Sabbath morning, as nearly as I can remember, a few days after our going on duty and the occurrences with Cronin which resulted in his leaving, it being the first Sabbath we were on duty at the White House, we were in a little waiting room on the right-hand side of the stairs. This room is now sometimes used by the President as a smoking room, and also as a reception room for those calling on the President and his family socially. Where the elevator now is used to be a pair of little old-fashioned stairs. You would go up a few steps and come to a landing; up a few more steps and another landing, and so on. This was a favorite stairway of Mr. Lincoln's, for he used it more than any other in the house. When he came downstairs that Sunday morning we were all chatting, and by "we" I mean Edward Burke, his old coachman, Edward McManus, Alfonso Dunn, and myself. When Mr. Lincoln came into the room he said, "Which one of you gentlemen will take a walk with me as far as Secretary Stanton's house? He is sick in bed and I want to see him." As I had seen a good deal of the world and had been placed with public men of high station, I immediately arose and said, "Mr. President, I will walk with you." After we had passed out of the front door and were still on the main portico, but out of the hearing of any one, the President said to me, "I have received a great many threatening letters, but I have no fear of them." I said, "Mr. President, because a man does not fear a

thing is no reason why it should not occur."
He replied, "That is a fact."

After we got off the portico, going east, I
said, "Mr. President, there has been many a
good, brave man who has lost his life simply
because he did not fear." Then he remarked
in a thoughtful way, "That is so; that is so."

Then we passed along out the eastern gate
and across Pennsylvania Avenue to Secretary
Stanton's house, which was opposite Franklin
Square on the north side of K Street, near
the late Senator Sherman's residence. It was
an elegant building. I stepped up and rang
the bell, and the servant who came to the
door admitted us at once. We were shown
into the private parlor, and the President said
to me, "Now you remain down here; I am
going upstairs into Secretary Stanton's room;
he is sick in bed." I said, "All right, Mr.
President." I picked up a book and passed
the time examining it until the President returned. On the way back to the White House
the President was silent a long time, thinking
of the grave problems of the day, I presume.

After a while he began to talk, and in the
course of the conversation I mentioned Senator Harlan, and said, "Mr. President, Senator

14

Harlan seems to be a very good man." He replied, "Yes, Senator Harlan is a good man." It always seemed to me a singular coincidence that very soon after this conversation Mr. Lincoln appointed Senator Harlan as one of his Cabinet officers. Afterwards Robert Lincoln married his daughter Mary, whom I knew very well, as I did also her mother and father.

Almost every day about ten o'clock I would accompany Mr. Lincoln to the War Department. He was exceedingly anxious about General Sherman's army, which was at that time marching through the South. On one occasion he remarked to me that he felt very uneasy about Sherman's army, since he had not been able to receive any information regarding it for three weeks. In going over to the War Department I used to try to expedite his leaving the White House as much as possible, because people would always hang around and wait to see Mr. Lincoln, and would thrust notes into his hands as he passed and in many ways annoy him. One day just as we got to the front door, after going out of the private corridor, there was a nurse who had been in the East Room with an infant in her arms and a little tot walking by her side. Just as we were about to pass out of the door, she got in front of us. I took hold of the little tot gently, and moved her to one side so that we could get out. The President noticed this action, and rather disapproved of my moving the child to let him pass and said, "That's all right; that's all right." The interpretation I put upon his words was that he would sooner have been annoyed by people thrusting letters into his hands than make a little child move aside for him to pass. When we did get out he started off rapidly. Mr. Lincoln did not seem to be walking very fast, but it kept me hustling to keep up with him; so much so that although I was pretty tall myself, I had a curiosity to know how tall the President was. One day as we were about to leave the White House, I asked the President his height. He replied, "I am just six feet three inches in my stocking feet."

During the Rebellion, the "Molly Mc-Guires" up in the State of Pennsylvania had been giving the Government a great deal of trouble, as a result of the officers endeavoring to enforce the draft which had been proclaimed all over the United States. These fel-

16

lows did, indeed, put our Government to a great deal of unnecessary trouble. The "Molly McGuires" were one of the toughest elements that ever infested the State of Pennsylvania. Many a good man was put out of the way by these roughs, and it could never be found out who committed the deed, or when or how it was done. Consequently, the Government had to put its strong arm down on these men. Quite a number of them were sent to the prisons. One day a number of people were shown into the President's office. Finally all left except two tall, gaunt Irish women, who were truly pictures of despair. They went up to Mr. Lincoln and said: "Howdy, Mishter President. We've cum to see yers, sir; to see if yers wouldn't pardon our husbands out of prison, sir." This was said in whining, woe-begone voices, and well-pretended looks of despair on their faces. "We would like to have yers pardon 'em out of prison, sir, so as to help support us, sir," they added, in wailing tones. The President sized them up. He was a great reader of human nature. Then, in the same identical twang the Irish women had used, he said, "If yers hushbands had not been resisting the draft, they would not now be in prison; so they can stay in prison." The two Irish women, without further words, turned away and left in double quick time.

I recall another incident that serves to show the gentle nature of the great President and what manner of man he was. There came to the White House one day another Irish woman. She was well advanced in years, and was accompanied by her little daughter, who could read and write, and who was a very bright little child.

She took a seat and waited for the President until he had finished with the other visitors. She then came forward with her little daughter. She was tidy and neat in her person, and very modest in manner. She said, "Mr. President, my husband is down sick at the hospital in Fredericksburg, and I would like to have him discharged, for yers have my husband and two sons, all three, in the army, and I need the help of one of them, either one of my sons or my husband." The President said, "You make an affidavit to that effect and bring it back to me." In the course of a day or so she returned again, and the President so arranged it that she could go down and take the order for the husband's or son's discharge. She had been gone probably three weeks, and the matter had passed out of my mind, when one day she returned to the White House. When she came up to speak to the President her voice was full of sorrow, and she was nearly crying as she said, "Mr. President, when I got down there he was dead. Now yers have two sons yet. I want to see if yer won't discharge one to help me get along, and yers can have the other one." Then the President said to her as he had done before. "You make an affidavit to that effect and bring it to me." She did so, and returned with the affidavit to the President. After he had arranged it so that she was to get one of her sons back, she stepped up to him and said, "Mr. President, may God bless you, and may you live many long years." After she had left the room and there was nobody in the office with the President but myself, he said to me, looking up into my face, "I believe that the old woman is honest."

One day an artist brought a painting of the President which he wanted him to see. I went in and said, "Mr. President, there is a man out there who has a painting he wants you to see." He replied, "Fetch him in."

The artist came tugging the picture in a large, heavy frame. He put it down and waited for the President to speak. It was considered quite a big thing for an artist to get the President's opinion of his painting. Mr. Lincoln looked at the picture for some time without saying anything. Then, with considerable humor in his eye, he said to the artist, "Why, yes, that is a very good picture of me, and do you know why?" The artist was all worked up at the President's attitude, and was so confused he could not reply. "Well," continued Mr. Lincoln, "I'll tell you why it is the best picture of me; it is the ugliest." The artist was rather taken back for a few moments, but went away perfectly satisfied.

Along about four o'clock one afternoon there were a number of people waiting outside to see the President. He looked up at me from his desk and said, "Pendleton, how many people are out there?" I replied, "Mr. President, there are quite a number." I shall never forget his next remark. He got up, came over to the window, looked at the crowd of people waiting, and then said, "Turn them in; turn them in," just like an old farmer used to say to me, "Tom, pull down the bars and turn in the cows."

One day a paymaster's wife came in, very stylishly dressed, and said, "Mr. President, I would like my husband to be relieved at the front and some other man sent in his place." Mr. Lincoln looked up, and said, "Madam, I cannot do that. It would necessitate sending another paymaster in his place, so he will have to remain at his post."

Another time a major called. He was anxious to get in to General Hancock's corps, then being organized. He told the President he would like to get in this corps, and left his papers with him. In the course of a few days he returned and reminded Mr. Lincoln of the fact of having left his application and requested a reply. Mr. Lincoln said to him, "Yes, I have read your papers, but I do not find anything very strong in them." "Why," said the major, "don't you see what General Hancock said?" "Yes," replied the President, "he says you are a gallant officer." "What more could you want him to say?" asked the major in surprise. "Why," replied Mr. Lincoln, "he does not say that you are a sober officer." The man carried signs of dissi-

pation on his face. He marched out of the
office with his papers under his arm, and that
was the last time I ever saw the pompous
major.

One day a number of persons were shown
into his office, and among them an old personal friend from Illinois. He at once came
up to Mr. Lincoln, shook hands with him and
said, "Why, Mr. President, you look just
about as you did when you were out in Illinois." Here was an opportunity for the man
to forget affairs of state and relax from business cares and the burdens, which at that time
were bearing heavily upon him. The President said, "Yes, I am about the same, and that
puts me in mind of an old farmer out in Illinois who had an old horse which he put in
pasture to recuperate. After the horse had
grazed in the pasture some time, one of the
neighbors came along and remarked to the
owner of the old horse, 'Well, you put this
horse in here to recuperate, but he looks just
about the same as when you first put him in
here. He neither recupes nor decupes.' And,"
added Mr. Lincoln, "that's just about the way
it is with me." The two friends then had a
very hearty laugh.

Under President Lincoln

One night, while sitting in the little ante-room, I heard the doorknob turn quickly and in walked Mr. Lincoln with his shoes in his hand, and said, "Now I caught you! Do you know what you put me in mind of?" "No, Mr. President!" I said. "Well, you put me in mind of a boy that got forty-three eggs in the barn and put them under a hen, and then came and told his mother that he had set a hen on forty-three eggs. She said, 'That cannot be true, for a hen cannot cover forty-three eggs.' 'Well, mother, I know that, but I just wanted to see her spread herself.' So I wanted to see how you would spread yourself."

In November, 1864, on the night of Mr. Lincoln's re-election, we started over to the old War Department. It was very different in those days from now. When the President wanted to consult any of his Cabinet members he would take a trusty guard with him, walk over to the office of the Secretary, and have a plain business talk with him. No matter whether it was day or night he would go personally. On the night in question, Major Hay, now the Secretary of State, was on the left side and I on the right of the President, as we went over to the old War Department.

23

That night he took a different course. Instead of going to the east door, he undertook to go across the grass and enter by the south door. In passing through this ground on several previous occasions I had noticed that pegs were driven in the ground and a telegraph wire stretched across them, in order to keep people from walking over the lawn. Mr. Lincoln wanted to go that way, but I suddenly remembered the pegs, and grabbed him by the arm, just as he was about to stumble over the wire, and said, "Look out, Mr. President." However, his foot did strike the wire, and in a few moments more he would have been sprawling on the ground, a very undignified position for a President, to say the least, but by grabbing him as I did I saved him from a heavy fall. "Well," said he, "I never would have thought of that." We then proceeded without further incident. When we reached the main entrance he went on with Major Hay, saying to me, "Now, Pendleton, you may return to the house, and I will get some of the people over here to walk back with me."

One day a man with a very swarthy complexion came in wearing a silk hat and a Prince Albert coat. You would have taken

him at first glance for a minister of the gospel.
He commenced finding fault with Mr. Stanton, the great War Secretary, accusing him
of not carrying out the order that President
Lincoln had given two weeks before to have
a certain man liberated from prison who had
been sentenced to death, but was pardoned.
Mr. Lincoln listened patiently to his com-
plaint, and then said, emphatically, "If it had
not been for me, that man would now be in
his grave. Now, sir, you claim to be a philanthropist. If you will get your Bible and turn
to the 30th chapter of Proverbs, the 10th
verse, you will read these words: 'Accuse not
a servant unto his master, lest he curse thee,
and thou be found guilty.' " Whereupon the
man got "huffy" and went away. But as he
went out, he said, angrily, "There is no such
passage in the Bible." "Oh, yes," said Mr.
Lincoln, "I think you will find it in the 30th
chapter of Proverbs and at the 10th verse."
This was late in the afternoon, and I thought
no more of the occurrence. Next morning I
was at Mr. Lincoln's office door as usual,
about 8 o'clock, and heard some one calling
out: "O Pendleton! I say, Pendleton, come
in here." When I went inside Mr. Lincoln

said to me, "Wait a moment." He stepped quickly into the private part of the house, through what is now the Cabinet Room, but which was then used as a waiting room, and soon reappeared with his Bible in his hand. He then sat down and read to me that identical passage he had quoted to the philanthropist, and sure enough it was found to be in the 30th chapter of Proverbs, and at the 10th verse.

In those days I was not much of a Bible reader. But in 1865 I decided that all-important question whether or not I should be a follower of the Lord Jesus. I commenced reading a little old Bible that I had bought at a second-hand store and which had belonged to an old soldier. After this I always kept it with me at the White House, and would occupy my odd hours in reading from it. One day I came across that same passage which Mr. Lincoln had quoted to the angry philanthropist. The whole occurrence came back to me, and I thought what a just man was the President. He was not even willing for me to be in doubt as to his correct quotation of a Bible passage, but must needs take his precious time to prove himself right in my eyes. How simple-hearted, yet how truly great a man he was.

On one dark Sunday, to the best of my recollection, in the month of December, Mr. Lincoln started with me over to the old War Department. He had lately been very much worried about affairs of state, and seemed this day to be lost in thought. We went in the east door, and then had to climb a stairway. The steps were not exactly winding, but had a couple of landings, and led to Secretary Stanton's door. On the way from the White House to the old War Department were a great many large, fine trees which were boxed, and I had often thought how easy it would be for a man to secrete himself behind one of them, wait for the President to pass that way, then jump out and kill him before the guard could prevent, though he might be ever so watchful. When we reached Secretary Stanton's office I stayed outside the door while Mr. Lincoln went in to see him. He remained a long time. When he was ready to return and came out of the door, I was by his side in a minute. We had walked down to the first landing, about half-way down the stairs, when we met a man coming up. He was thick-set, and wore a gray suit of clothes. The man scrutinized Mr. Lincoln very closely, and I had my eye on him all the time. The President did something very unusual for him— he looked at the man very steadily, as if trying to fix his features on his memory. Before the man reached the upper landing he turned and took another look at the President, and again Mr. Lincoln and I both looked at him. After we got out of the building, where there was no one near us, the President said to me, "Last night I received a letter from New York stating that there would be a man here who would attempt to take my life. In that letter was a description of the man who was said to be anxious to kill me. His size and the kind of clothes he would wear when he would make the attempt were carefully described. The man we just passed agreed exactly with the description given me in that letter."

On one occasion when quite a number of people were shown into the President's office, there was among them a young girl, rather timid looking, as though she had come from one of the small towns or a rural district. There was evidently something weighing very heavily on her heart. I supposed her brother, uncle, or some of her kindred who were probably in the army, had been ordered shot, or that she had some other trouble which bore very heavily upon her. When she got before the President, poor thing, she was so embarrassed that she could not open her mouth. The President saw the situation, and at once, in his kind, fatherly way said, "Now take a seat just over there, and after a little while I will see you," and presently did so.

On one occasion there was no one in the room but little Tad Lincoln and myself. An old-fashioned settee and some rickety chairs constituted the furniture. Those were the days when we were not thinking about furniture. Little Tad piled two or three chairs upon the settee and secreted himself behind it. Just as the President came in, Tad pitched the chairs and settee over into the middle of the floor in front of his father. The President roared out laughing. Sometimes when we would come from the War Department and pass through the same little room, little Tad would be there, and he would put his great arms around the little fellow and tug him off upstairs.

Mrs. Kendall, Mr. Lincoln's bosom friend,

relates a sad incident which came under her observation one day as she came from the East Room. She saw over on one side of the room a young girl weeping as though her heart would break. She went over and asked her what was the trouble. The young girl said, "Oh, madam, my brother is to be shot and I cannot get to see the President!" Mrs. Kendall asked to be given the papers, and upon receiving them, she immediately went upstairs and saw the President for the young girl. She stated the case, and gave him the papers. Probably he examined them. At any rate, he said to her, "You go downstairs and tell the girl to go home and give herself no uneasiness about her brother. It will be all right."

During this period there was one of my companions, Alfonso Dunn, who was in a good deal of trouble. Some of his relations had been drafted—two men—and each one of them had families and could not raise money enough for a substitute. Their wives were very much distressed to think they would have to go to the front. Dunn said to me one day, "Tommy, won't you go upstairs and see Mrs. Lincoln and ask if these men may have more time in which to get a substitute?" I said,

"Dunn, why don't you go up and see her yourself?" He said, "Tommy, I don't like to go."
He pleaded with me so earnestly that I finally
went upstairs and saw Mrs. Lincoln for him.
She told me to go in and see the chief clerk
and have the document drawn up; then I was
to bring it in to her, and she would sign it. I
did so, and before the ten days expired peace
was proclaimed. Consequently, Alfonso was
happy and the two men who would otherwise
have been compelled to leave their wives were
also happy, I presume.

There was a company of "Bucktails" down
in the White Lot, south of the President's
mansion. It was a rough, rugged looking
place then, and these fellows were encamped
there. Little Tad was very fond of them. He
would go down and mix among the camp
fires when the men were cooking their grub,
and get his face all black with soot and come
home dirty. His mother would scold him,
and have him all nicely washed and dressed,
and he would come down where I was to talk.
"Tom Pen, I would like to go to the theatre
to-night. Won't you go upstairs and ask
mamma if I can go?" I would go to her and
say, "Mrs. Lincoln, won't you let Tad go to

the theatre to-night?" And she would say, "No." Then I would plead with her and say, "Now, Mrs. Lincoln, let him go." "Will you go with him, Pendleton?" "Yes, madam, I will, and take good care of him." "All right, Pendleton; then he can go." Sometimes he would say to me when we were going on one of these trips, "Tom Pen, have you got any money?" I would say, "Yes, Tad," and I would lend him some money. He was like other boys, fond of sweet things, peanuts, apples, and the like. The little fellow was always very honorable in paying back whatever little amount he would borrow from me.

On one occasion, President Lincoln, when riding near the Soldiers' Home, said to his footman, named Charles Forbes, who had but recently come from Ireland, "What kind of fruit do you have in Ireland, Charles?" To which Charles replied, "Mr. President, we have a good many kinds of fruit: gooseberries, pears, apples, and the like." The President then asked, "Have you tasted any of our American fruits?" Charles said he had not, and the President told Burke, the coachman, to drive under a persimmon tree by the roadside. Standing up in the open carriage, he pulled off some of the green fruit, giving some of it to Burke and some to Charles, with the advice that the latter try some of it. Charles, taking some of the green fruit in his hand, commenced to eat, when to his astonishment he found that he could hardly open his mouth. Trying his best to spit it out, he yelled, "Mr. President, I am poisoned! I am poisoned!" Mr. Lincoln fairly fell back in his carriage and rolled with laughter.

This story was afterward told by the coachman, justifying himself upon the grounds that it was too good to keep.

After the fall of Richmond, while we were all rejoicing and happy to think that the long war was nearly over, the order came to illuminate the White House. It fell to my particular lot to do all the lighting up. In those days we did not have any electric lights, and the job was a tedious one. First, strips of wood were nailed to the windows, and on these pieces of wood were placed small pieces of tallow candles. There were tiers and tiers of them, lighting the entire front of the White House. Then I had to stand guard to see that none of the candles set fire to the window curtains and the inflammable decorations. We were all happy that night.

In the month of November, 1864, Mr. Dana, Assistant Secretary of War (long years after this well-known as the editor of the *New York Sun*), and Mr. Lincoln had an interview at the White House on a Sabbath morning, after which they left together for the old War Department. After they had transacted their business, we started over to the old Navy Department. I kept a short distance behind them, because I did not want to overhear their conversation. As soon as they entered the building the doorkeeper slammed the door to, with a bang, in my face. In an instant it was opened again, and Mr. Lincoln told the doorkeeper that it was all right and to let me in. We separated after they finished their business, and I accompanied Mr. Lincoln back to the White House.

In the same year, during the month of November, there was a great crowd assembled in front of the President's Mansion. I stood up at the window by Mr. Lincoln, and held a candle in my hand while Mr. Lincoln delivered his address. The majority of his listeners were soldiers. I thought while he was delivering that address how easy it would have been for some assassin to have killed him with an air gun. Afterwards Henry Ward Beecher addressed this multitude of people, and the crowd then dispersed.

Mr. Lincoln's last inauguration was held on Saturday night, after he had been re-elected as President of the United States. There was a lady from England, a personal friend of Secretary Stanton, who wished to see the President and shake hands with him. Mr. Stanton had her sent to the White House in his private carriage. When she got out of the carriage the multitude of people was so dense on the portico that it was almost impossible for her to get to the main entrance. She was nearly crushed to death. Unfortunately there was some man with his heavy boot right upon her foot. I was in the little waiting room on the right-hand side of the entrance looking after the wraps and hats of the diplomats and officers when a knock came at the door. There were two gentlemen with this lady who had rescued her from this terrible jam of people. They said to me, "Will you kindly let this lady be brought in here?" I said, "Certainly." She was in a fainting condition. After she was brought in I closed the door, and the gentlemen retired. I immediately got some water, took my handkerchief, and while she lay on the settee bathed her temples. I continued doing so until she appeared to feel better. In the meantime, I left her in the sitting room, and crowded my way through the hallway where the jam of people was very compact, into the Blue Parlor, with a glass of water for Mr. Lincoln. He drank it, and seemed to enjoy it very much. The perspiration was just rolling down his face as he grasped the hands of the passing throng, as though he had been splitting rails as of yore. After the lady had thoroughly recovered and the reception was nearly over, she went in and had a grasp of the President's hand. Everything passed off very nicely that night, and next morning, the Sabbath, Simon Cameron called upon the President.

Mr. Cameron was received in the Blue Parlor. After awhile they came out and stood in the grand corridor opposite engaging in earnest conversation. The President said, "Cameron, something occurred to me last night at the reception that never did before." He held his hands up and said, "Cameron, between every one of these fingers is a blister from the shaking of hands." After one term in the White House, and numerous receptions, the President had never experienced anything like this before. It was probably due to the interest felt in him on account of the great events of the day.

On Thursday evening, December 29, 1864, Mrs. Lincoln had one or two notices written to be sent down to the daily papers in regard to a New Year reception she would hold. She wanted them published at once. She handed them to Edward McManus, the doorkeeper of the White House, with instructions to take them to the local papers at once. This he failed to do. Probably a half or three-quarters of an hour passed before Mrs. Lincoln had occasion to come through the main corridor again. When she did so, she approached Edward and asked him about the notices. "Why, Edward," she said, "I told you to take them to the newspaper offices at once. Now, this is the last duty you will ever perform in the White House." He treated this statement very lightly, and smiled a sickly kind of smile. But it was indeed his last day. Next morning early Mrs. Lincoln sent for me, saying she wanted to see me in the private part of the house. When I went up there she told me she wanted me to resign my position and take charge of the front door—to take the place of Edward McManus. I told her I could not do this unless I was regularly appointed to the duty. She told me to go up to the Capitol and see Mr. French, the Commissioner of Public Buildings and Grounds, and tell him to make out my appointment as doorkeeper of the White House. I went to see Mr. French, but he declared that this appointment was not in his power to make, as it was made directly by the President. So I returned, and in the course of the day I had an opportunity to speak to the President. I said, "Mr. President, would you have any objection to my taking the place of Edward McManus?" He said, "None at all." That evening, after nightfall, on Saturday, it being the last day of the week, month and the year of 1864, I was up near the door of the President's office when little Tad came along and said, "Tom Pen, give me that paper. Come on in now to papa's room." The President was sitting at the table facing the east. Tad said, "Papa, dear, do me a favor?" Out he handed my ap-

38

pointment. "Sign this for Tom Pendel." He laid it down on the table, and the President took up his pen and endorsed the appointment. And that appointment holds good to this day.

On the fourteenth day of April, 1865, in the evening, just previous to the time when the President and Mrs. Lincoln were going to the theatre, George Ashmun, of Massachusetts, called on Mrs. Lincoln, and I showed him into the Red Parlor, took his card upstairs, and soon the President and Mrs. Lincoln, with Mr. Colfax, then Speaker of the House, came downstairs and went into the Red Parlor, where Mr. Ashmun was waiting. They all entered into a lively local conversation, and came out of the Red Parlor presently, and stood in the inner corridor. Their conversation was about the trip Mr. Colfax proposed to take across the continent. They then passed out of the corridor into the main vestibule, and stood in the main entrance, where they again chatted. Mr. Colfax bade the President and Mrs. Lincoln good evening, and went upstairs to see the Private Secretary, Mr. John G. Nicolay. Mr. Ashmun went out on the portico with the President and Mrs. Lincoln,

said good-bye, and started off downtown.
Ned Burke and Charles Forbes, the coachman
and footman, respectively, drove over to a
private residence, and took in the coach Major Rathbone and Miss Harris, who was the
daughter of Senator Ira T. Harris, of New
York.

Previous to starting for the theatre, I said
to John Parker, who had taken my place, to
accompany Mr. Lincoln, "John, are you prepared?" I meant by this to ask if he had his
revolver and everything all ready to protect
the President in case of an assault. Alfonso
Dunn, my old companion at the door, spoke
up and said, "Oh, Tommy, there is no danger." I said, "Dunn, you don't know what
might happen." Because I had traveled a
good deal in my life, and had seen much of
human nature, I said, "Parker, now you start
down to the theatre, to be ready for the President when he reaches there. And you see him
safe inside." He started off immediately, and
did see Mr. Lincoln all safe inside the theatre,
and Mrs. Lincoln, Major Rathbone and Miss
Harris also reached the building in safety.

What transpired after they left for the theatre may be of interest, so I will mention the

incidents occurring at the White House during their absence.

About ten o'clock, as nearly as I can remember, one of the sergeants of the invalid corps, who was doing duty around the White House, rang the bell, and I stepped to the door. He said, "Have you heard the news?" I replied, "No." He then said, "They have tried to cut the throat of Secretary Seward." He lived in a house close by where the Lafayette Theatre now stands. I said to him, "O Sergeant, I guess you must be mistaken!" I supposed he referred to the accident that happened to Mr. Seward three weeks before this. He had been thrown from his carriage, and his jawbone had been broken in the fall. The sergeant went away to his post and returned in about fifteen minutes. He rang the bell, and I stepped to the door again. He said, "I tell you that it is a fact; they tried to cut Secretary Seward's throat." Then I began to feel very uneasy about the President.

Probably he had been gone this second time twenty minutes, when I saw quite a number of persons hastening towards the White House through the east gate. Men, half-grown boys and small boys all seemed to be in a great hurry. Some of the boys were running. When they arrived at the door, the central figure was Senator Sumner. He came to inquire about the President. I said, "Mr. Senator, I wish you would go down to the theatre and see if anything has happened to the President." They hurried away just as fast as they had come. Probably about twenty minutes before eleven o'clock, I stepped up to the door in answer to another ring at the bell. Who should be there but Isaac Newton, the Commissioner of Agriculture. This is now a Cabinet position, but was then a commissionership. I admitted him inside the door, and at once closed it. He was a bosom friend of President Lincoln. I was thoroughly acquainted with him, and I knew to whom I was talking. He said to me, "They have shot the President. And the bullet," he said, "has enered the left side of his head." I immediately hurried upstairs, leaving him on the inside, and went to Captain Robert Lincoln's room. He had just come from the front that morning, where he had been doing duty on the staff of General Grant.

That room was directly over the front portico. When I got into his private room, he did not seem to be feeling very well, and had a vial in one hand containing medicine and a teaspoon in the other, as if he was about to take a dose of medicine.

As I stepped up to his side the teaspoon and the vial seemed to go involuntarily down on the table, and he did not take the medicine. I wanted to approach him gently and break the news to him about his father. So I simply said, "Captain, there has something happened to the President; you had better go down to the theatre and see what it is."

He said to me, "Go and call Major Hay," who was in the room now used by Secretary Cortelyou. That was Mr. Nicolay's and Major Hay's bedchamber at that time. I said to him, "Major, Captain Lincoln wants to see you at once. The President has been shot." He was a handsome young man with a bloom on his cheeks just like that of a beautiful young lady. When I told him the news, he turned deathly pale, the color entirely leaving his cheeks. He said to me, "Don't allow anybody to enter the house." I said, "Very good, Major. Nobody shall come in." They took their departure immediately for the theatre. They had been gone probably half an hour, when poor little Tad returned from the National Theatre and entered through the east door of the basement of the White House. He came up the stairway and ran to me, while I was in the main vestibule, standing at the window, and before he got to me he burst out crying, "O Tom Pen! Tom Pen! they have killed papa dead. They've killed papa dead!" and burst out crying again.

I put my arm around him and drew him up to me, and tried to pacify him as best I could. I tried to divert his attention to other things, but every now and then he would burst out crying again, and repeat over and over, "Oh, they've killed papa dead! They've killed papa dead!"

At nearly twelve o'clock that night I got Tad somewhat pacified, and took him into the President's room, which is in the southwest portion of the building. I turned down the cover of his little bed, and he undressed and got in. I covered him up and laid down beside him, put my arm around him, and talked to him until he fell into a sound sleep.

Ah! that was a sad night for the nation, and to me it was simply awful, for I loved Mr. Lincoln probably better than I loved any one else in all the world.

While I was putting little Tad to bed other men had taken my place at the door, but after he went to sleep I returned to my duty.

Two hours after his death his body was escorted to the White House by a squad of soldiers. Funeral services were held in the East Room on the 19th of April. Rev. Dr. Hall, of the Church of the Epiphany, read the burial service; Bishop Simpson, of the Methodist Church, offered a prayer, and Rev. Dr. P. D. Gurley, Mr. Lincoln's pastor, delivered a short address on the courage, purity and faith which had made the dead man great and useful. The coffin was then carried to the funeral car, and amid the tolling of all the bells of Washington, Georgetown and Alexandria, and the booming of minute-guns from several batteries, moved to the Capitol, where it lay in state until the morning of April 21, when it was taken to the station. At 8 o'clock the train, decked in sombre trappings, moved out toward Baltimore. Governor Brough, of Ohio, and Mr. John W. Garrett, of Baltimore, were in general charge on the sad journey.

The train arrived safely in Baltimore, and

there I saw more weeping and grief-stricken people than in any other city through which we passed. We dined in Baltimore, and then had a procession, after which we left for Harrisburg. There we had a procession, and his remains lay in state all night in the Capitol. Next morning preparations were made for the trip to Philadelphia, where we arrived about four o'clock in the afternoon. A procession was formed immediately, and it must have been at least nine o'clock before we could leave our carriages. It can well be imagined that about this time we were all greatly fatigued. If I remember correctly, the remains of Mr. Lincoln lay in state in Independence Hall, and three red lights were kept burning there all night. The people moved in silent procession through the building all night long to view the body. All day Sunday, and until three o'clock Monday morning, great crowds of weeping people passed in mournful procession to take a last look at the beloved hero.

We left Philadelphia for New York, and arrived at quite an early hour. Here the throngs of people were immense, and the police had all they could do to keep the great mass back, so

that the procession could pass up to the City
Hall, where the remains were laid in state.
The decorations in New York City were
something wonderful, particularly on Broad-
way and Fifth Avenue, where they were of
the finest materials. On the day of the departure of the train from New York there must
have been fully half a million people viewing
the procession. We left from Twenty-ninth
Street and went to Albany, arriving at an
early hour in the morning. Another procession was formed, after which Mr. Lincoln's
body was laid in state in the Capitol.

We next stopped in Buffalo, where we had
the usual procession. The building in which
his body was placed was guarded by members
of the Continental Guard, in old Continental
uniforms, who kept watch all through the
night. Our next stopping place was Michigan
City, where we were greeted by thirty-five
young ladies, who stood on the platform and
sang a beautiful hymn. They were all dressed
in white, and presented a fine appearance.
We left there quite early in the morning and
proceeded to Indianapolis. Here, after the
procession, the remains were laid in state and
were viewed by throngs of people all day Sun-

day. On Monday morning we left for Chicago.

We arrived safely and the body lay in state in the City Hall all one night and day. After we arrived there was an immense procession formed to escort the body to the City Hall. The mass of people who came to view the remains was immense.

A little incident connected with this trip might be interesting to note here.

I met a young lady who had passed through to look at the body of Mr. Lincoln, and she was so much hurried that she did not get more than half a glance at him. The building in which he lay in state stood in the centre of a large square with an iron railing all the way around it. The people had to pass at once out of the gateway and could not return again. This young lady seemed to regret so much that she had obtained so slight a view of the great President's face, that she asked me to help her get another look. I said to her, "You come this way." I showed my card of invitation issued by the Secretary of War, and we were immediately admitted to the inclosure. Then we passed up through the building again, and she got a better opportunity to

48

look in the President's face, and seemed very grateful to me for helping her. I asked if she would like to look at him again. We passed right around the building, I showed my card and was again admitted, and this time she had a still better opportunity to gaze on that face still in death. After we returned to Washington this young lady wrote me one or two letters, and seemed to feel very grateful for the little kindness I had been able to show her. We then left Chicago, and started for Springfield, Illinois, the home of Mr. Lincoln, where he was to be finally laid to rest.

There was some friction as to where he should be buried. Two parties seemed to be in charge of the arrangements, one contending for his burial in one place, and another maintaining he should be laid away in a very different place. Finally the party holding out for the cemetery prevailed, although in the city limits, where the second party wanted him buried. The other vault was nearly finished, and they were working on it like a lot of bees.

When everything was at last settled and ready, the great final procession was formed, and the last march was commenced to the burial place of this great man.

After the funeral, preparations were made for our return trip. We arrived in Washington on Sunday morning, having been absent over three weeks. We found that President Andrew Johnson had taken up his quarters in the west wing of the Treasury Building, as he did not wish to disturb Mrs. Lincoln, who was still in the White House. She left with her son Robert in the latter part of May, and that was the last I ever saw of her and poor little Tad.

Some years after, during the Hayes administration, a Mrs. Rathbone called on the President and his family. I met her as she was leaving, and found that she was the Miss Harris who was in the box with Mr. Lincoln the night he was assassinated. She had just returned from Ohio, and said that Mrs. Lincoln was living there, in a town called Poe. She stated that Mrs. Lincoln requested her to inquire how many of the old employees were still in the White House. It touched me much to think that Mrs. Lincoln did not forget her old employees. I never saw Mrs. Rathbone after this.

Andrew Johnson.

CHAPTER II

UNDER PRESIDENT JOHNSON

Mrs. Lincoln finally completed her arrange-
nts and left the White House, as nearly as I
1 remember, about the first of June.

President Johnson, with his staff, then
ved into the Executive Mansion.

Those who came with him were General
azzey and Colonel ~~Morrill~~, who were on his
ff; Lieutenant Long, and Colonel Brown-
r, his private secretary.

The death of two of these officers was very
gic. Colonel ~~Morrill~~, long years after-
rds, in the city of San Francisco, blew out
brains with a revolver. He was one of the
ghtest young men it was ever my fortune to
et in the White House.

Colonel Long, also many years after this,
d to frequent the White House. One day
ile there he said to me, "Mr. Pendel, my
e wants you to talk with me." While one of
: Army and Navy receptions at the White

House was in progress, I did have an opportunity, which I used to talk to him. He was very kind-hearted and listened attentively to all I said. His great weakness was a love of strong drink. I called on two occasions at his house. I read the Word of God to him, and knelt down and prayed with him and his family. His wife was a very nice lady indeed, and he had two charming little children. He seemed to be somewhat affected by my interest in his behalf. The next time I met him, at his home, was the last time I ever saw him alive. His wife was sick in bed. I did not get to see her at that time, but I had a long talk with him, warning him of his danger, and he again listened attentively to me. I said to him, "Colonel, won't you try to stop this business?" "Oh," he said, "what do you mean, Mr. Pendel?" I said, "Colonel, you know how Colonel Morrill ended his life." As I said that, he stood with his back to the mantel and I was facing him. I said, "Colonel, be careful. You may end your life in the same way." "Oh, no! I will never do that, Mr. Pendel," he said. Ten days after this, he took his revolver and died the same death as Colonel Morrill. It was very sad, very sad, indeed.

52

Under President Johnson

After President Johnson had been some time in the White House, a fine present came to him from New York City. This was a splendid span of horses and a fine carriage. It was a gift to the President from some parties in New York City. With it came a letter. The President very respectfully declined this gift but retained the letter, because he had a suspicion that there was something behind it all. After he had been in the White House quite a while, the President made a trip which was called "swinging the circle." He was gone from Washington for some time. While he was away, Mrs. Senator Patterson, his daughter, received an invitation from Mrs. General Grant to attend an evening party which was given in the upper part of Georgetown. At this time the President had not yet purchased a new carriage and horses, and the Postmaster-General very kindly offered his own vehicle, horses and driver to Mrs. Patterson and her children, to convey them to this party at Mrs. Grant's home. Along about sundown, Mrs. Johnson sent for me to come up to her rooms. She was very delicate in health, but a very kind-hearted lady, indeed. She said, "Mr. Pendel, I wish you would go over to Mrs. Grant's and remain there until the party is over, and see Mrs. Patterson and her children safely home." I went over to Mrs. Grant's house and presented myself with the message from Mrs. Johnson to Mrs. Grant, who said, "Why, you are not going to take her away already?" I said, "Oh, no, Mrs. Grant; certainly not until the party is over. I came simply to see her safely home after the party." While I was waiting, she sent me some refreshments.

After the President had procured his carriages, there was a tall Frenchman who attended to the horses. I think he came from Canada. The President on one occasion had got up quite early in the morning, and happening to look down towards the Potomac River, saw Nicolas with his carriage and horses moving through the White Lot very rapidly downtown. He had the circumstances investigated, and it developed that Nicolas, the Frenchman, was in the habit of going out early in the morning with the carriage and picking up passengers wherever he could find them! That was the last drive in the President's carriage this Frenchman took, you may be sure. He was hustled out in double quick

54

time and was soon looking for another job, which I hope he secured.

On one occasion a member of one of the foreign legations called on Mrs. Stover, the other daughter of the President. She respectfully declined to see him, but Mrs. Patterson went down and saw him. Mrs. Stover did not care about doing any of the receiving, so her sister, who was in reality the Lady of the White House, did all the honors of the house; hence she responded to this call.

At one of Mrs. Patterson's drawing-room receptions, the Commissioner of Public Buildings and Grounds, Mr. French, failed to appear. After she had waited a suitable time and he still did not come, and quite a number of the guests were in the grand corridor waiting to be presented, she sent for me. I had the pleasure of presenting all the ladies and gentlemen to Mrs. Patterson at that time, and she said to me, after it was all over, "Mr. Pendel, you did that very nicely, indeed, and seemed quite used to making presentations."

Andrew Johnson's last reception was one of the largest I think I ever saw. There was a crowd that passed through the state dining-room. I noticed a lady throw up her hands in that great jam of people—in a few moments more she would have fallen to the floor, and more than likely would have been trampled to death.

When I saw the situation I hurried to her assistance, and with all the strength I had (which is a good deal more than I have got to-day) it was as much as I could do to pull her out from that mass of people. After she had rested some time, and the crowd had thinned out a little, I think she went in to shake hands with the President. It is perfectly wonderful what the people will undergo and suffer in order to shake hands with the President at one of the great White House receptions.

At one of the private dinner parties which President Johnson gave, Mrs. General Michler was one of the specially invited guests. She came out through the grand corridor, and into the main vestibule, and said she was very sick. I immediately drew a chair up to one of the windows so that she could get the fresh air, and even then she was so ill that she fainted dead away. I hurried up and got some cold water with which I bathed her temples and face thoroughly, using my handkerchief.

Under President Johnson

Presently she regained consciousness and seemed much improved.

The Queen of the Sandwich Islands dined with him at one time during his administration.

One day during Mr. Johnson's administration, probably after three o'clock in the afternoon, a surgeon of the army, in full uniform, called to see the President on business. I let him pass into the East Room and he handed me his card. While I was talking to him, and telling him it was after the hour for visitors, one of the President's grandchildren, Miss Stover, a girl of about twelve years of age, whipped the card out of my hand and put off to her grandfather with it. I never was more deceived in a man in my life. He seemed to talk in a perfectly rational manner, with no sign in the world of insanity. The President pretty soon came down and said to me, "Why did you send these cards to me?" I said, "Mr. President, I did not. Mrs. Stover's little girl snatched them out of my hand and carried them to you." He asked, "Where is the man?" I said, "In the East Room, Mr. President." He said, "Show him in here." (In the grand corridor.) As soon as the man got a sight of the President he showed his insanity to the full extent. I soon had him out of the White House, and he went off down the street very peacefully.

During this administration the conservatory took fire and was totally destroyed. Many valuable plants were lost, among others one which was said to have been owned by General Washington.

I recall that one day Mr. Johnson gave a birthday party to three hundred boys and girls, the occasion being his own birthday. The state dining room was literally loaded with good things to eat, and the children certainly had a glorious time. My daughter and son, who are now living, received invitations, and well remember the joyous festivity. Although not invited, various grown persons, mostly females, made an excuse to bring the children, and did not forget to load themselves with bonbons until their pockets bulged.

The President honored me one New Year's Day during his administration by asking me to dine with him. I accepted his invitation, but, though he subsequently gave me many invitations, I thought it best to decline, and dined with him only on that one occasion.

I think President Johnson placed a good deal of confidence in me. When a vote was taken in the District of Columbia to see if the citizens were in favor of the colored men voting, some one went to the President and told him of it. He was told that I was one among a very limited number who voted for the enfranchisement of the negro. This was a falsehood. I did not vote at all on that question. The man who carried this falsehood to the President was told by him, when he had finished his tale, "Mr. Pendel is a man who always attends to his business." That settled the question with this tale-bearer.

A young lady, a personal friend of the President, on one occasion dined and spent the evening at the White House with the family. About half-past nine in the evening Mr. Johnson sent for me to come up into the library. The young lady was there with the rest of the family. He asked me to see the young lady safely home in his carriage, which was waiting at the door. I did so, and afterwards returned in the President's carriage to the White House.

Probably about the middle of his administration his impeachment trial was brought up. Judge Bingham was the prime mover in it, if I remember rightly. The President had a very able lawyer to represent him, and the result, as all the world knows, was an honorable acquittal, thus relieving the President and the country of a great anxiety.

The day that he was acquitted tables were spread in the library and wine and cigars were served. Some of the employees drank to excess. I was invited up from the front door, but soon went down to my business.

President Johnson was a very generous man. He used to have a table set in the room which is now used by the steward, and here meals were prepared, and the doorkeepers and the help about the house did not have to go out to luncheon. No other President ever did this to my knowledge, either before or since the time of Mr. Johnson.

Mrs. Patterson was a very nice lady and did the honors of the White House in a way acceptable to every one with whom she was brought in contact. Her husband was at that time Senator from Tennessee, and the entire family resided at the President's mansion.

Under President Johnson

The family consisted also of a son, and daughter, Mrs. Stover, with her two daughters and a son (small children); Robert Johnson, the oldest son of the President, then his private secretary, and Frank Johnson, the younger son. Out of that entire household there lives to-day only Mrs. Patterson and her son Andrew, both of whom reside in the neighborhood of Greenville, Tenn.

CHAPTER III

Under President Grant

The first inauguration of General Grant was a grand affair.

On the evening of the fourth of March, long after the procession had all passed, a youth in West Point uniform, with three or four friends, came to the front door and commenced moving in. I stopped him and told him the house was closed to visitors. He said, "I am General Grant's son Fred." I said, "All right, then, sir, you and your friends can pass in."

General Grant brought all his staff officers with him. General Rollins, chief of staff; General Dent, his brother-in-law; General Horace Porter, now Ambassador to France; General Comstock; General Badeau, who wrote the "Memories of Grant;" and General O. E. Babcock.

Throngs of people besieged the White House day after day, so persistently that they had to have a guard chain put on the inside of the door, in order that we could open it just wide enough to talk to the people outside, and find out what they wanted before we attempted to let them in.

After the General had been in the White House some time, as President, and things got to running smoothly, the crowd thinned out considerably, so that the President could take a walk. One evening on his return I opened the door for him and he said, in a very quiet way, "I think that fastening could be taken off the door now." I said, "All right, Mr. President, it shall be attended to at once." And it was. General Grant and Mrs. Grant were certainly very popular with the people, and the number of people who called on them, socially, in the evening, was simply wonderful.

Quite a number would call regarding their petitions for office. A lady and gentleman came from the South. They gave me their cards which I took up to the President, but he begged to be excused from seeing them. There was something very peculiar about that couple, I thought. After I had delivered the message to them—the lady was a very fluent talker—I entered into a conversation with her. She talked very rapidly, and moved her position frequently; first, she would be in a chair and sit there a few moments; then she would sit down on a sofa, and then to the chair again, talking incessantly all the time to me, and I to her. Her next move was a very peculiar one. There was a large, heavy marble-top table standing in the waiting-room, on the right-hand side of the entrance; she went up to the table and first sat on the edge of it, then kept edging up, further and further, until she had both feet upon the table, and was sitting right in the middle of it, talking for dear life all the while. It was to me one of the most astonishing sights imaginable. After talking a long time, she and her escort took their departure very quietly, and seemed to be perfectly happy as they went out.

On one occasion some company called on Mrs. Grant in the afternoon. There were several ladies and gentlemen in the party. I took their cards up to Mrs. Grant, who was in the library at the time, and the President was sitting at the piano, thumping the keys with one hand. I presented the cards to Mrs. Grant, and she said, "Ulysses, shall we see these people?" He replied, in that dry way of his, "Mrs. Grant, that's your funeral, not mine," and they had a good, hearty laugh over it. She finally went down to see the callers for a short time.

When General Sherman or General Sheridan called on the President, he was always heard to say, "Why, Sherman, how do you do?" or, "Why, Sheridan, how do you do? Come in and be seated." There was no formal "General" about it, but just the address of familiar friendship.

One day I saw two gentlemen coming up the sidewalk. It was after three o'clock in the afternoon. I said in my mind, "I do not think the President will see these two gentlemen." I stepped to the door and met them, and said, "Gentlemen, it is after the hour when the President receives visitors." They said, "We have an engagement with the President." I said, "All right, gentlemen, if that is the case, walk in." I went into the inner corridor, and there met the President, who had just lit a cigar, and was about to take his evening stroll. I said, "Mr. President, these two gentlemen say they have an engagement with you. I told them it was after your hours for receiving visitors." The President immediately spoke up and said, "Yes, I had an engagement with them at two o'clock; it is now after three o'clock, and I must poke my nose out of doors a bit, to get a little fresh air." He said to me, "Where are the gentlemen?" I said, "In the little waiting-room, Mr. President." He stepped to the door and they met him immediately, and he said, "Gentlemen, your engagement was for two o'clock; it is now after three, and you failed to fulfil your engagement, and I must have a little opportunity to poke my nose out of doors, and get some fresh air. Good afternoon, gentlemen," and the President walked out, smoking his cigar.

On another afternoon, as the President started to take his walk, a woman met him on the portico, and her tongue commenced running at a great rate. If she didn't rattle it out at the rate of ninety miles an hour! The President listened to her very attentively, and when she had about run down, as a clock would, she handed him a letter. He said a few words to her, put the letter in his pocket and continued his walk.

Another time when President Grant had been out walking—the day was very gloomy, it looked as though a northeast storm was brewing—the rain commenced pouring down in torrents just as he entered the east gate on Pennsylvania Avenue. He did not hasten his gait a particle, but seemed to enjoy the drenching he was getting, and walked along as unconcerned as though the sun was shining and such a thing as rain was never heard of.

One evening Jesse Grant had "Jeff Davis" brought up to the house—this was a little black war horse the President used to ride in battle. He started off for his ride. After he had been gone some time "Jeff Davis" came scampering home, and no rider on his back. After a while Jesse came trudging home on foot. In the meantime, the President saw "Jeff Davis" making his way towards the stable, and Jesse and he met in the main vestibule. Considerable dust was on Jesse's clothes. The President, in a laughing way, said, "Why, Jesse, where is 'Jeff Davis?'" Jesse said, "I don't know. He threw me way out there in the dust, and put out for home." The President had a hearty laugh over this incident.

Jesse used to like to come and sit in the little anteroom, and talk to me about men-of-war. I would tell the different parts of a man-o'-war and what the sailors on board had told me, and he seemed to take quite a fancy to me. He was very much like his father in his ways —very quiet in his manner of speaking. He took a seat in the room alongside of me one day and said, "Mr. Pendel, you don't smoke." I said, "No." He said, "You don't chew." I said, "No." He said, "You don't drink." I said, "No." He said, "Good man! good man!" I afterwards related this incident to his wife, as I was taking her through the conservatory, and she had a good laugh over it.

Miss Nellie Grant was a charming young lady of a most pleasant disposition—very pleasant and quiet. Always, when she would be going to a dinner party, evening party, a ball or a dance, I was at hand with her wraps, to put them on for her. I was very fond of her, and she was always very polite and kind to me. One evening an old tramp had got in the south grounds. He followed Miss Nellie and her young friend, Miss Annie Barnes, up the south portico steps. Pretty soon they hurried in and told me what had happened, and I went out and brought Mr. Tramp into the main vestibule and sent for the police officer who was out in the grounds. I said to Miss Nellie,

"I am going to have him arrested." "Oh," said she, "I must see that, as I never have seen a person arrested." She and Miss Annie Barnes seemed much interested in the proceedings. The officer came and put the tramp under arrest, and took him off. He was, apparently, a German.

Miss Annie Barnes and Miss Nellie Grant were great chums. Miss Barnes lived right opposite the White House where the French Ambassador now lives, on H Street, between Seventeenth and Eighteenth Streets N. W. She would spend a great many evenings with Miss Nellie at the White House, and would take dinner there often. After dinner, Miss Nellie would come to the glass door and I would be at the main entrance; she would say, "O Pendleton [like Mrs. Lincoln used to do], come here a minute! What time do you go home?" I said, "About half past nine in the evening." "I want you to see Miss Annie Barnes home." "All right, Miss Nellie, I will do so with pleasure." Then she would say, "Now, Pendleton, don't forget; let us know when you are ready to go." Miss Annie Barnes was the daughter of the Surgeon-General of the United States Army, and a

very pleasant, lively young lady she was, too.
She is now dead.

One night, while the President was at dinner, quite a fine looking young woman, well-dressed, came up to the door and wanted an audience with the President. I saw very soon that she was mentally unbalanced. I thought that possibly she was of Scotch descent—she was very persistent in trying to get an audience with the President. Finally I got her away by telling her she would have to come some other time, as the President was at dinner and would not see any one that afternoon. That seemed to satisfy her and she went away.

One Christmas Eve they were all sitting in the library. The President sent for me to come there. He handed me two notes. The first one he told me to take to Mr. Galt, the jeweler; the second one, to Mr. Steinmetz, the furrier. I took the first note down and gave it to Mr. Galt. They were quite busy in the store, it being Christmas Eve. He read the note, and he scrutinized me thoroughly up and down. He read it over the second time—if I remember rightly. He said, "Did General Grant send this note?" Said I, "He did." He looked at me with some suspicion, then wrapped up and handed me a case, about the size of a letter, filled with gold lockets. Then I started out. "Now," said I, "I have more than I bargained for, to take care of all this jewelry." Then I went to Mr. Steinmetz, who knew me very well. In Galt's they did not know me at all.

They filled out the order for some very nice furs, and wrapped them up and gave them to me. I got on the car and felt very uneasy about the jewelry, on account of the number of people on the car. When I went upstairs and delivered the two packages, I said to Mrs. Grant, "The man down there in Galt's looked very suspiciously at me," and she laughed heartily. After they had examined the lockets thoroughly (I don't remember whether the General made any selections or not— probably he did), he handed them back to me, and said, "Go down and tell Mr. Galt to send up some others, that I want to examine them further." When I got there the second time there was no scrutinizing, but he very readily handed me out the lockets, and I went to the White House with them. After the President made his selection, I returned the rest to Mr. Galt.

Under President Grant

General Grant was a remarkable man. He displayed more patience than any President I ever saw in the White House. Once he came downstairs to take a drive in his buggy. The buggy was not there. He smoked his cigar, and waited and waited. He walked up and down the portico, and would "right-about" in regular army style, and walked up and down, and smoked again, and after waiting until the patience of an ordinary man would have been worn out, Albert finally appeared. Instead of railing out at Albert for his slow appearance, he said something pleasant to him, took the reins and drove off.

Mrs. Grant was a very pleasant lady, indeed. She was very kind-hearted. There came to the White House after dinner one evening a young man who was a stranger here who had been robbed and thrown down an areaway near the City Hall the night before. He seemed to be very anxious to see Mrs. Grant, and I got to talking with him and found out, to a certain extent, what his trouble was. I went up and saw Mrs. Grant and she listened to me while I explained the situation to her; then she said, "Go down and find the particulars from him, and how far

from home he is now, and let me know." I
went down and did as she told me, and went
back and told her all that the young man said
for himself. I think then she further said,
"Find out how much money it will require to
take him to his home." I did so and reported
to her. She handed me enough money to pay
his fare back to the West. I came down and
gave it to him and he went away happy.

On one Sunday afternoon quite a number
of boys were playing around the old fountain
in the south grounds, near where the Marine
Band gives its concerts now. One of the
larger boys took off the hat of one of the
smaller, and threw it in the fountain. Mrs.
Grant hurried down to me and said, "Pendleton, go down and get that little boy's hat out
of the fountain; he is crying for it." I started
down, but before I got there one of the other
boys had picked the little fellow's hat out, and
they all scampered away in haste at sight of
me.

During General Grant's administration, his
daughter, Miss Nellie, was married to Mr.
Algernon Sartoris, as everybody remembers.
The wedding was a grand affair. She was
married in the East Room, right in the centre

of the three windows on the east side. There was a beautiful marriage bell suspended over her head. The four large columns supporting the girders were all entwined with the beautiful National colors. Palms and other plants were artistically placed about the room, the windows were closed, and the room was brilliantly lighted. The effect was beautiful in the extreme. The procession formed upstairs in the western portion of the building. There were twelve bridesmaids. All marched down the grand stairway in the west end of the building, through into the East Room where, as I said before, the ceremony took place. There were about three hundred invited guests. In a line with the grand corridor there were a naval officer and an army officer on one side and a naval officer and an army officer on the other side, who held blue and white ribbons parallel with the white pillars, up to where the ceremony took place. After the ceremony was all over the invited guests repaired to the Red Parlor; that is, the ladies did, and I had the pleasure of presenting to them the wedding cake—put up in little white boxes about six inches long and three inches wide—for them to dream on, that those who were single might dream of their future husbands.

After Miss Nellie had sailed for Europe, one night after dinner the President took a walk downtown, and everybody had left the house with the exception of Mrs. Grant, Jerry Smith, the old colored duster, and myself. When the President had been gone probably fifteen minutes, Mrs. Grant, who was sitting in the Blue Parlor, seemed very lonesome. She called me away from the front door to come in near the Blue Parlor door and be seated, as the house was perfectly deserted except for us three. While I was sitting there the conversation turned to Miss Nellie. I said to her, "I am very sorry, Mrs. Grant, that Miss Nellie has gone away. We all miss her very much." Mrs. Grant spoke up and said, "Yes, and we will have her back home again." I chatted with her until the President returned and then took my post again at the front door.

During his term in the White House the President returned from Long Branch unexpectedly, one evening very late. He called me upstairs into the office, which is now used as the Cabinet Room. He had be-

fore him a great pile of papers to be signed.
He had pulled off his coat and hat and was
trying to keep cool, as the weather was intensely hot. As fast as he would sign one of
these documents I would move it aside in order to give him a chance to sign the next one,
and so on. He said to me, "Pendel, I wish
you would go over to the home of the Secretary of the Treasury, Mr. Boutwell." It was
situated where the Shoreham Hotel stands
to-day. I said, "Mr. President, there is no one
at the door but me to-night; what shall I do,
go down and lock the door, and put the key in
my pocket?" "Yes," said he, "that will keep
everybody out." I started at once to Mr.
Boutwell's house, and when I got there and
rang the bell, everybody was out, and the
house all shut up. I returned to the White
House, unlocked the door, and went up and
reported to the President.

General Grant was certainly a grand man.
The day of his second inauguration was one
of the coldest days I ever felt here. The West
Point cadets had been ordered to Washington
to take part in the inauguration parade. They
had marched up to Washington Circle, past
the Executive Mansion, and in so doing—it

was intensely cold and they had no overcoats on—one of them was freezing to death while in the ranks. Word of this fact came to the White House and Mrs. Grant heard of it. She had the young man brought over to the White House immediately and I put him to bed, covered him up nice and warm, gave him a strong stimulant, and Mrs. Grant said to me, "Now, Pendleton, I want you to look out for this young man and take good care of him." Late in the afternoon, after the procession was all over, he came around all right so that he was able to get out of bed, and I went down to the hotel with him. Mrs. Grant was very kind-hearted. She had as good care taken of this young man as if he had been her own son.

Mrs. Grant, in holding her drawing-room receptions would always have me stand in the Blue Parlor, ready, in case she should want to give an order of any kind when she came down. Sometimes she would come downstairs and forget her handkerchief. "Pendleton, go upstairs and bring me down a clean handkerchief," she would say. She seemed to be quite forgetful of the little articles that go to complete a toilet for receiving. Sometimes she would forget her white kid gloves, and,

"Pendleton, go up and get me a pair of gloves," would be the order. Then I would have to hunt up the dressing maid, who was usually, about this time, down in the basement taking her dinner; and so it would go. The maid would not want to stop eating her dinner to go up and get the gloves called for, so she would say to me, "You go upstairs, and look in such and such a drawer, in the dresser in Mrs. Grant's room, and there you'll find the gloves."

Sometimes she would forget her fan; sometimes it would be her ear-rings, and almost invariably, when she would come downstairs ready for her receptions, I would have to skirmish upstairs and try to find what she required, in case I could not induce the maid to go.

One day the General had been out in the hot, broiling sun, and when he returned he was pacing up and down in the grand corridor. The perspiration was rolling down his face, and he had his handkerchief out wiping it off. He was so warm that his handkerchief was soon saturated. I stepped up to him and said, "Mr. President, let me take that handkerchief, and go upstairs and get you a dry

one." I hurried upstairs and soon returned
with one that was nice and dry. He seemed to
be gratified at the attention, and continued
walking up and down the corridor.

The President had a very spirited pair of
horses and a fine buggy. One day he and
Mrs. Grant came down together and I helped
to assist her into the buggy and they started
off at a pretty rapid gait. They hadn't been
gone a great while, when they returned also
at a pretty rapid pace—so rapid that Mrs.
Grant was rather afraid to sit behind the
horses the way the General had them going.
I assisted her to alight from the buggy and the
General then went driving by himself, and you
should have seen how he put those horses to
their full speed. Every one thought it was a
case of runaway, sure.

On one occasion the President gave a dinner party. The "big guns" of the Republican
party were the guests—Senators and members of Congress. I recollect Roscoe Conkling
came in, and quite a number of other Senators. I would show them into the little waiting-room, assist them off with their wraps,
show them into the Red Parlor, hurry upstairs
and announce their arrival and names to the

President. Finally a certain Senator came in; when I went upstairs to announce his name to the President, I left him in the anteroom, but did not show him to the parlor. When I announced his name the President seemed to be very much taken aback. "What!" he said, upon hearing his name, "are you sure?" "Yes, Mr. President, I am sure." He said, "Go downstairs again." Down I came to the little waiting-room, and said to this Senator, "I believe this is Senator ——?" "Yes, that's my name." I went back and reported to the President. He seemed to be very much embarrassed. I never saw him so much embarrassed at any time as he was that night. He said, "Go and call the Secretary." I did so, and they had a conference about the Senator downstairs. He then told me to go downstairs and tell Senator Conkling and one or two others to come up to him. They, too, held a conference about the Senator in the waiting-room. Mrs. Grant was called into consultation also. After a time, when they seemed to have come to a satisfactory conclusion, the President said, "Show him into the Red Parlor." They all passed in to dinner, and I don't suppose up to the time of the

Senator's death, he ever dreamed of that conference as to whether he should be admitted or not—for he was a red-hot Democrat, and the others were all high Republicans.

At another dinner party there were quite a number invited to whom regular invitations had been sent, and among the guests were a gentleman and his wife who were stopping at the National Hotel. He was promptly on time, but the lady was disappointed on account of the fact that her dressmaker had not finished her dress for that evening, as promised. After they had all gone into dinner, her carriage came driving up at a breakneck speed. I hurried out on to the portico and assisted her out of the carriage; she asked if they had gone into dinner. When I told her they had, she seemed very much embarrassed indeed, and exclaimed, "Oh, what shall I do; what shall I do?" I said, "Madam, don't be worried, it will be all right." That seemed to encourage her and I showed her into the waiting-room at once, then into the Red Parlor as quickly as I could. I hurried into the private dining-room and announced her at once. Col. Fred Grant got right up from the table and stepped into the Red Parlor, and she took his arm very gracefully. The ice was thus broken and the embarrassment all over, and she said afterwards she never enjoyed a dinner party more than that one. It passed off very satisfactorily to everybody.

On another occasion there was a state dinner given. Simon Cameron, a United States Senator, the father of Don Cameron, also, as you know, a Senator many years afterwards, was one of the invited guests. The guests had all arrived except Mr. Cameron. They had waited a suitable time for him and were about to start into the state dining-room from the Red Parlor. The President said to me, "When Senator Cameron comes, bring him into the state dining-room, and give him a seat opposite to me." After they had been seated at the table probably half an hour, the Senator made his appearance and had a long hickory staff in his hand. I said, "Mr. Senator, just walk this way," and immediately showed him to the seat kept for him. He wasn't bothered at all about this breach of etiquette, but took things quietly; he sat down to the table and commenced to do justice to his dinner.

One of the most notable occasions was when the King of the Sandwich Islands dined with

General Grant. He sat on the south side of the table in the state dining-room. There was something transpired the night of that dinner which I never saw before in the White House. The King had three valets, and the chief one you might term his cup-bearer. Those men, all three of them, stood right at the King's back. The chief valet, or cup-bearer, as the courses were served, would take the dishes and pass them to the King. All three of these men wore what you might call regalias, and they were in the shape of ladies' Bertha capes. It certainly was a singular scene in the estimation of an American.

At another time during the Grant administration there was a state dinner given. Quite a number of members and Senators were invited. There was a new member invited on that occasion whom I had never seen before. I asked him if he had ever met President Grant. He said he had not. The President and Mrs. Grant were waiting in the Blue Parlor where they received the guests. I asked him his name, and he gave it to me. Then I presented him with a diagram of the table and showed him where he would be seated. I escorted him then into the Blue Parlor, introduced him to the President and Mrs. Grant, who made him feel perfectly at home. He soon mingled with the crowd, and seemed to be perfectly satisfied. On the occasion of Mrs. Grant's drawing-room receptions my position was always in the Blue Parlor, near Mrs. Grant and the President. While one of these receptions was going on, in marched a big double-fisted Dutchman, with his breeches jammed into the top of his raw-hide boots. After he passed by the receiving line, he stepped over to one side of the drawing-room, and dropped down on one of the elegant sofas. Mrs. Hamilton Fish, wife of the Secretary of State, was assisting Mrs. Grant and other ladies in receiving. She said very quietly to me; "Will you please have this man leave the room." I stepped over to him and said very quietly, "Won't you walk into the Green Parlor?" He got up and hustled out, and that was the last I saw of him. During one of General Grant's evening levees, General Michler, who was then Commissioner of Public Buildings and Grounds, failed to put in an appearance at the proper hour. Consequently, when the people began to gather, I began to introduce them to the President. I presume I had presented a hundred people to the President, when General Michler made his appearance. Then my duties of introducing ceased, and I took my former position near President and Mrs. Grant.

Just an evening or two before the close of the Grant administration, a great many callers, personal friends, came to say goodbye. Among them were some ladies, and as they were about to take their departure, one of them remarked, "I suppose, Mrs. Grant, you are very glad that you are going to leave the White House?" She replied, "No, I am not." The President and Mrs. Grant were very popular while they were in the White House. The social calling was something immense in the afternoon, and especially in the evening, when I would often have to go into the Blue Parlor and bring chairs into the Red Parlor to seat their friends.

During this period Fred Grant, his son, was married, and they made the White House their home for quite a while. Their first daughter was born there, who is now the wife of a Russian nobleman. Mrs. Fred Grant was very handsome. She was just as pretty as a picture. She is the sister of Mrs. Potter Palmer, of Chicago, who is also a very handsome woman. After they left the White House at the close of the administration, they became the guests of Hamilton Fish, Secretary of State during the Grant administration. Upon the outgoing of the Grant and the incoming of the Hayes administration, the ex-President had so many handshakings and good-byes to say, and we were all so busy, that I didn't have an opportunity to shake hands with him, and to say good-bye. The second day after he had gone away from the White House, as nearly as I can recollect, I called on him, was shown into the parlor and had an opportunity to have a good handshake and a good-bye. I then thanked him for his kindness to me during the administration. I didn't see General Grant any more after that until he had made his trip around the world. I called on him again when he returned to Washington. He was then the guest of General Beall, at the corner of Seventeenth-and-a-half and H Streets, which now fronts on Lafayette Square. On this occasion I took my autograph album with me, and the General gave me his autograph.

The last time I saw General Grant alive was one Saturday afternoon I met him in the main vestibule of the White House. He said to me, "I would like to take a look at the East Room." I said, "Certainly, General, walk right in." After he came out I said, "General, would you like to take a look through the parlors?" He said, "Yes, I would." After I showed him through the Green and the Blue Parlors, we entered into the Red Parlor. There was in it a very fine portrait of Chester A. Arthur. After he looked at it awhile, he turned to me and said, "Who is the artist that painted that?" I said, "That is by LaClair, of New York, an American artist of French descent." He said, "Oh, yes! He is a very good artist. He is painting a portrait for me now." And that is the painting which is now hanging in the main corridor, leading to the Blue Parlor. It is full life-size, and the best portrait I ever saw of General Grant. A singular incident this, that after he had been President of the United States for eight years, I should be showing him around through the White House.

Under President Grant

Mrs. Grant's father, Judge Dent, in the 85th year of his age, died in the White House, in one of the chambers overlooking the northern portico. His remains lay in state in the Blue Room. He was a thorough Democrat out and out.

CHAPTER IV

UNDER PRESIDENT HAYES

Directly after the inauguration, when they had all returned to the White House, and those who could get in had been in and paid their respects to President and Mrs. Hayes, I picked up her wrap, and started upstairs from the Blue Parlor with her and the President. When we got upstairs, I started to show them the various chambers in the house —bed-chambers, etc. After I had showed them all the bed-chambers, we went into the library, which is directly over the Blue Parlor. It is an oval-shaped room, the same as the Blue Parlor. We proceeded into the Cabinet Room, and I explained that to them, and from that into the President's office, and showed them the rest of the official part of the house, in the meantime introducing them to all employees who were at that time connected with the official household. They then returned to the private part of the house, and rested themselves a little while; then their friends commenced calling upon them, and continued doing so until ten o'clock that night, and we were all very tired when we got through. The next day there were a great many delegations called on the President, and with ladies calling on Mrs. Hayes, we had our hands full that day. In the course of the day the Glee Club of Cleveland, Ohio, called on the President and Mrs. Hayes, who came down to receive them in the Blue Parlor. When the members had been introduced and had shaken hands with them, they stepped out into the main corridor right opposite the Blue Parlor, and sang that grand old hymn, "The Sweet Bye and Bye." The President and Mrs. Hayes both enjoyed it very much. I did, extremely so, for it did my soul good. I shall never forget that hymn as sung upon that occasion. The clubs, military organizations, and delegates continued to come, and the social calling was so great in the masses of people who called. Mrs. Hayes was a grand lady, and the White House will never have one to surpass her. After they got settled down and the crowds had left the city, I then had a better opportunity of finding out the character of both of them. And the character of both was beautiful! As she would be going out to breakfast through the upper corridor of a morning how often I have heard her singing a beautiful hymn. How kind-hearted she was. Always had a kind word to say to the humblest employee at the White House. Notes would come to the White House time after time from the destitute and poor wanting help. She would have me come upstairs and see her, and would say, "Mr. Pendel, here is some money, and here is a note. Take this, and find out where they live, and give it to them." On one occasion, out on Massachusetts Avenue, there was a young girl, about twenty-two years of age, down with consumption, and Mrs. Hayes said to me, "Mr. Pendel, I want you to take these oranges up to that young lady and give them to her." The doorkeepers at the White House fared well, for hardly an evening passed but we were told to go into the parlor, and take that magnificent bouquet that was standing there. It was during this administration that General Hastings and Miss Platt were married in the Blue Parlor, under a beautiful marriage bell. It was a very quiet, but a beautiful

93

wedding. During the administration they gave the largest banquet in the White House that I ever saw given. Three thousand invitations were sent out, and twenty-five hundred accepted. The state dining room was set with small tables laden with a bounteous repast, as were also the tables in the private dining-room, and after these banquets, everybody would go away happy. During this administration my wife and I celebrated the twenty-fifth anniversary of our marriage. Mrs. Hayes presented us with a half dozen beautiful silver teaspoons, and a sugar spoon lined with gold. Mrs. General Hastings also presented us with a beautiful silver butter knife in a handsome case lined inside with beautiful white satin. I have them at my house and can assure you I am very proud of them.

When they first came to the White House, their youngest son, Scott Hayes, was a little chap running around. Miss Fannie was a little girl. Webb Hayes, and Burchard, and the other son (I cannot recall the name) were all older than Scott. The young people used to have a fine time. Since that time Miss Fannie has matured into womanhood, and married a naval officer. I called upon her once when

94

she was residing in the Navy Yard, and had
the pleasure of looking upon the interesting
little baby, of which she seemed to be very
proud. She was very much like her mother in
her disposition, being very affable and pleasant. Scott Hayes has long since matured into
manhood, and is very handsome and gentlemanly in his manner. Their whole administration was very pleasant indeed. Sometimes
I would be showing strangers through the
house and would come upon Mrs. Hayes un-
awares in the Red Parlor. I would almost
invariably introduce these ladies and gentlemen to her, and they would go away very
happy. On one occasion the steward of the
White House, Mr. Crump, lost his little son.
I had gone out to see him, and while I was
there addressing the father, the President's
carriage drove up, and Mrs. Hayes came in,
saying, "Why, Mr. Pendel, how do you do?"
just as friendly as though she had been one of
my own sisters. After she had conversed with
Mr. Crump and his wife, and looked at the
little son, who was dead, and was about to
take her departure, she said, "Mr. Pendel,
come out and get into the carriage, and I will
take you down to the White House." I

thanked her very kindly, and told her I was
off duty, and was on my way home, in a different direction.

Toward the close of their administration
the callers increased. For the last two days
I had never seen anything like it. There were
more weeping people when they were about
to say good-bye than I ever saw in the White
House in all my life, and at the outgoing of
their administration, and the incoming of the
Garfield administration, I was so very busy
that I did not have an opportunity to shake
hands with either the President or Mrs.
Hayes. They became the guests of Senator
Sherman, Secretary of the Treasury, and of
Mr. Sutton. The next day I went over and
had the pleasure of meeting the ex-President
and Mrs. Hayes. That was the last time that
I ever saw her. President Hayes called at the
time poor Garfield was suffering at the White
House from the effects of being shot, and that
was the last time I ever saw him.

During President Hayes' administration
there was a newspaper man who used to slash
into him right and left, through the paper
with which he was connected, in the most
abusive way. The President did not know

who it was at the time, but after he left the
White House there was a commission appointed to go and visit the different prisons
throughout the United States. I think Mr.
Hayes was the president of this commission.
He visited quite a number of prisons, and
sometimes would talk with the prisoners.
One day while visiting some prison, I do not
know where, he got into conversation with
a man, a prisoner, who recognized ex-President Hayes, and there he told the ex-President, "I am the man, sir, who abused you so
fearfully in the newspaper, and, General
Hayes, I want to ask your pardon and forgive-
ness, for I did you a great wrong." What he
had been sent to the penitentiary for, I cannot
say. The President said to him, "Do you
ever have an opportunity to do any writing
in the prison here? If you do, send it to me,
and I will have it published in some magazine,
and I will send the proceeds to your wife and
children to help support them while you are
in prison." The man was taken aback at the
ex-President's kindness to him, and I think
afterwards Mr. Hayes succeeded in having
this man pardoned.

CHAPTER V

Under President Garfield

The incident most indelibly impressed upon my mind during the Garfield administration is, of course, his untimely and tragic death. I give here the official bulletins.

Preparations for the Worst

Second Dispatch.   (The midday bulletin.)

Long Branch, N. J., Sept. 19, 11.45 a. m.— The President's chill this morning was sharp and severe. Unless the chills can be controlled there is but little hope held out by the doctors. Dr. Boynton has just said, "While the case is not hopeless, I have no hope that the President can recover." Much excitement prevails here. All the doctors in the case are despondent.

Third Dispatch.

President's condition is critical.

L. of C.   99

Fourth Dispatch.

Early risers here were gladdened this morning by the statement from Attorney-General MacVeagh that the President had had a very comfortable night, but while the doctors were preparing the bulletin, they were suddenly called to attend the patient, who was found to be suffering with a severe chill, which lasted fifteen minutes, and was followed by profuse perspiration.

At 11 o'clock he was quietly resting. MacVeagh said to a friend, "The President grows weaker. We are more anxious."

Dr. Boynton said he would be apt to rally from this chill, but there was very little ground for hope of his recovery. Dr. Bliss says that the doctors agree that the original trouble is the wound, the consequent trouble is blood poisoning, which caused pus formation on the lungs. His rigor, they say, proceeds from his debilitated system. Dr. Agnew says that when they opened the abscess in the parotid gland he felt that the beginning of the end had come. He is reticent, but it can be noticed by his manner that there is no hope. The surroundings at Elberon are dismal enough; sorrow sits on every face, and people talk low and walk slowly as in the presence of death. Each word from the sick room is eagerly caught up, and the gloom deepens as time progresses.

Fifth Dispatch.

Dr. Boynton thinks there is danger of sudden death. The President fully aware of his condition.

Sixth Dispatch.

A recurrence of chills dreaded. Dr. Agnew expects the President will be unconscious many hours before death. Members of Cabinet disheartened.

Seventh Dispatch.

The doctors astonished at the President's vitality.

Eighth Dispatch.

Next to hopeless.

Ninth Dispatch.

Dr. Agnew does not expect death to-day. The President spent a quiet night, on account of his extreme exhaustion. The morning rigor accompanied by vomiting.

THE VICE-PRESIDENT READY

New York, Sept. 19.—Vice-President Arthur remained in his house all morning, receiving but few callers. A reporter called on him, but the Vice-President declined an interview, sending word that he had received nothing but the official bulletins. He had previously stated that he was ready to obey any summons made by the Cabinet, and he hoped that the President's strong constitution and the careful nursing he received would enable him to resume his executive duties.

Boston, Sept. 19.—Hon. R. T. Lincoln, Secretary of War, left Northampton, N. H., for Long Branch this p. m. He has hopes of the President's recovery.

About noon to-day Attorney-General Mac-Veagh telegraphed the War Department as follows about the President:—"Another chill at 10.30, and outsiders look for death at any moment. Doctors try to dispel this feeling, but without avail." A few minutes later the following dispatch came also from the Attorney-General: "Chill still continues. Pulse now 140, and growing weaker."

Under President Garfield

Effect of the News

There is no longer any hope existing in the public mind for the recovery of the President. Even those people here in Washington who have hitherto maintained a blind faith in a happy issue of this national sorrow, now abandon all hope. The general expectation is that the news of the President's death will be received before many more hours. Every heart is grieved. There is a gloom over the entire city. Business is almost at a standstill, and the nation awaits with bated breath the sad tidings which are inevitable.

Word was received at noon stating that Mrs. Garfield abandoned all hope. This broke the faith of even the most sanguine that the President would recover. The prevailing feeling seemed to be that if Mrs. Garfield, who had been so strong in her faith all along, gave up, then, indeed, there was no hope. As the afternoon wore on the excitement, which was itself subdued, increased. The crowds began to grow large around the posted bulletins. The general feeling was that the end would come within twenty-four hours.

Eleventh Dispatch.

Long Branch, N. J., Sept. 19, 2 p. m.—At
2 p. m. the President's condition remains un-
changed, and the physicians do not look for
another rigor until this evening, when one is
expected.

Twelfth Dispatch.

Long Branch, Sept. 19, 2 p. m.—The President is sleeping, and seems to be in a stupor.
He grows weaker, but may rally to-morrow,
unless he has a chill to-night. There is no
hope for recovery felt, but the doctors say it is
simply a question of time.

The Vice-President has not as yet been
summoned, but is kept informed of the President's condition.

DEAD

A Nation Mourns for James A. Garfield, Its Stricken President

*He Passes Peacefully Away, After Suffering
Terribly for Eighty Days—The Sad Event
in all its Detail.*

To-day the mighty nation will lift up its
voice and weep, for the long battle for life is

ended, and the President is dead. Peace and rest have come in mercy to the sufferer, with whose pains the people have suffered all the sad and weary days and nights for many weeks past. His services to his country are written in its history, and the honors bestowed on him by his neighborhood, his State, and the Nation attest the place he held in the hearts of the people.

His wife and children sit in the darkness of a grief which cannot be assuaged. May the Father of all Mercies give them comfort in their affliction.

For all time to come, Americans will mourn the untimely end of James A. Garfield, while the liberty-loving people of Christendom will do honor to his memory.

A second time in the history of the Republic is the Nation called upon to mourn the loss of its Chief Magistrate at the hands of an assassin. In the case of the lamented Lincoln, the infamous crime was surrounded with dramatic incidents, and occurred at a time when there was some excuse for unbridled passion. The shooting of President Garfield can be traced to no other cause than the wild act of a man either surcharged with malice or crazed by his own misfortune. The mourning of the people for his untimely taking off is genuine and sincere. Men of all shades of political opinion grieve at his loss, and the deep feeling of horror at the atrocious crime and detestation of the assassin is not confined to the personal or political friends of the dead President, but is universal.

He was President over the whole land; his life was the property of the whole people. His afflicted family have the sympathy and condolence of a whole nation, and for the delicate woman who is now a widow tears will be shed by strong men and noble women in every village and hamlet in the Union.

Special to *The Republican.*

Long Branch, Sept. 19.—The President died at 10.35. It came like a stroke of lightning. There was scarcely any warning. About twenty minutes before the event, he was found to be suddenly and swiftly sinking. Restoratives were sent for in all haste, and all the attendants were summoned. It was too late. It was in vain. Almost before the full group and the medicine came, he breathed his last. The correspondents engaged a whole force of carriages, and were driven, pellmell, to the Elberon. They got there just in time. In two minutes after their arrival on the stoop, Warren Young came slowly walking over to the hotel from the cottage. "What is the news?" "It is all over," he said; "he is dead."

It justified the familiar metaphor. It was a stroke. Death is always sudden, but rarely a more complete surprise than in this case. There had been a pyæmic chill in the morning, to be sure, of such a significant character as to cause Dr. Bliss to say the next in the series might be fatal. But as the day wore on without further incident, he seemed easier and brighter, and something like hope fluttered up out of despair. Dr. Bliss met the journalists with a good deal of his characteristic assurance. He took pains, however, to say that he did not mean to take an optimistic view, and did not wish to be understood that there was an improvement. Still, there was a negative gain in a stationary condition. The evening therefore began quietly. All immediate danger seemed over. Dr. Boynton had said, indeed, that death was possible to-night, but he did not regard it as probable. The correspondents made their plans to cover a remote contingency, and began on their stories of the day. At ten o'clock, therefore, the Elberon Hotel was almost deserted. The scene about the cottage was dark and lonesome; the stars shone dimly; it was very murky, and the heavy surf beat like a cataract on the beach. The President was lying quietly with the nurses who watched by his side. They were General Swaim and Colonel Rockwell. Dr. Boynton was also near at hand.

Suddenly the attack came, and in a few moments the awful danger of death loomed up before the attendants. The colored help was dispatched with all speed to call the doctors, and get a few necessary articles.

The commotion did not escape the newspaper sentries. Inquiries were hastily made, and the fact discovered that a mortal crisis was at hand. The next moment it was flashed over the country, while the great body of correspondents were summoned by telegraph to their quarters at the West End Hotel, nearly two miles distant. The operator dashed out of his little closet by the hotel door, too much excited by the news to state it plainly, but before it was posted the tidings had spread, that the President was rapidly sinking, and all the doctors had been summoned to the bedside. All that could be learned was that a messenger had been sent for mustard, and that another had gone to summon the doctors. It was evident that a sudden and unlooked for crisis had come. What it was, we could not for the moment know, but some one was pretty sure to come from the cottage before long, and until then we must be patient. Soon an under-secretary of the White House force, who had been one of the President's attendants here, came out and was met by the reporters. "What's the matter?" was eagerly asked. The secretary, Mr. Warren Young, was silent, and walked on two or three steps without replying. At length he said, "It's all over." The voice was gentle and the tones were low, but those three words were in one minute more heard from one end of the country to the other. The scene which followed the announcement was one of a lifetime. There was an instant cry of woe and horror. No one had dreamed of such news. At the worst we supposed it was another chill. "Dead! Dead! Dead!" went from one to

another in a whisper. A nervous shudder
went through the crowd. Then someone,
alive to journalistic duty, started at full speed
for the telegraph stand, in the adjoining
office of the hotel. His motion was conta-
gious, and the next instant there was a wild
rush for the wire lattice of the office. "You
can't file anything," shouted the operator,
"the Government has taken possession of the
wire." There was nothing else to do but to
rush to the West End.

By Associated Press. Long Branch, Sept.
20.—Previous to his death, the only words
spoken by the President were that he had a
severe pain in his head. It is supposed by the
surgeons that death was occasioned by a clot
of blood forming on the heart. Dr. Bliss was
the first one notified of the President's expres-
sion of pain, and upon entering the room he
at once said that the end was near. The members of the family were immediately summoned to his bedside. All arrived, and perfect
quiet prevailed, and Mrs. Garfield bore the
trying ordeal with great fortitude, and exhi-
bited unprecedented courage. She gave way
to no paroxysms of grief and after death became evident, she quietly withdrew to her

own room. There she sat, a heartbroken widow, full of grief, with too much Christian courage to exhibit it to those around her. She, of course, was laboring under a terrible strain, and, despite her efforts, tears flowed from her eyes, and her lips became drawn in her noble attempt to bear the burden with which she had been afflicted. Miss Mollie was, naturally, greatly affected, and bursts of tears flowed from her eyes, notwithstanding her noble effort to follow the example of her mother.

The death scene was one never to be forgotten. Perfect quiet prevailed, and there was not a murmur heard while the President was sinking. After death the body was properly arranged by Dr. S. A. Boynton. Telegrams were immediately sent to the President's mother, in Ohio, and to his sons Harry and James, who are now at Williams College; also, to Vice-President Arthur, and other prominent men. Eugene Britton, of Long Branch, the coroner of Monmouth County, will hold an inquest over the body of the late President. He has as yet made no arrangements for the inquest, and, as far as can be ascertained, he has not yet been notified of the President's death. The body will be embalmed and an autopsy will take place tomorrow afternoon. Dr. Curtis, of Washington, has been asked to come here in company with the attending surgeon, who recently withdrew from the case, namely, J. K. Barnes. J. J. Woodward and Robert Reyburn are to be present when it is made.

Arrangements for the Funeral

will be made in all respects in accordance with the wishes of Mrs. Garfield. Nothing has yet been definitely determined upon, but it is expected that a special train will leave here on Wednesday, for Washington, and the President's remains will lie in state in the rotunda of the Capitol during Thursday and Friday. On Friday evening, it is expected that the body will be taken to Cleveland, where it will lie in state during Sunday, and the funeral will take place on Monday. The place of interment will be Lake View Cemetery, at Cleveland, in accordance with the frequently expressed wish of the President in his lifetime. Of course the arrangements are subject to alterations.

Attorney-General MacVeagh says that Mrs. Garfield is bearing her affliction with the fortitude with which she has borne her trials so long, and is as well as could possibly be expected under the circumstances. The following telegram was received by Attorney-General MacVeagh:

New York, Sept. 19.

Hon. Wayne MacVeagh,

Attorney-General, Long Branch.

I have your telegram, and the intelligence fills me with profound sorrow. Express to Mrs. Garfield my deepest sympathy.

CHESTER A. ARTHUR.

Elberon, N. J., Sept. 20, 2.30 a. m.

The following has been received from New York:

Wayne MacVeagh, Long Branch.

Please convey to the bereaved family of the President my heartfelt sympathy and sorrow for them in their affliction. A Nation will mourn with them for the loss of a Chief Magistrate, so recently called to preside over its destiny. I will return to Long Branch in the morning to tender my services if they can be made useful. U. S. GRANT.

The Cabinet Announce His Death

Long Branch, Sept. 20, 12.25 a. m.—Attorney-General MacVeagh has just sent the following to Vice-President Arthur:

It becomes our painful duty to inform you of the death of President Garfield, and to advise you to take the oath of office as President of the United States without delay. If it concurs with your judgment, we will be very glad if you will come here on the earliest train to-morrow.

William Windom,
　　Secretary of the Treasury,
William H. Hunt,
　　Secretary of the Navy,
Thomas L. James,
　　Postmaster-General,
Wayne MacVeagh,
　　Attorney-General,
S. J. Kirkwood,
　　Secretary of the Interior.

Steward Crump's Story
The Dead President—An Interesting Incident of His Life.

Steward Crump was found late this morning, sitting in the hall at the foot of the east stairway of the White House, and surrounded by nearly all of the attachés of the White House who are now in the city. He had heard the awful news of the President's death through *The Republican* extra, which he had heard the boys crying on the streets, just as he was going to bed. At two o'clock a. m. he had received no dispatches from Mr. Brown or Colonel Rockwell, but expected to do so at every minute, and intended remaining up all night. He said that the house can be put in complete order for the reception of the President in a couple of hours, should the remains be brought here. The East Room is yet in complete order, and only a portion of the rooms downstairs have been cleared out. Mr. Crump was much distressed at the sad news, and said that he had had all the time the strongest faith that General Garfield would get well. He said, "He was always so cheerful and had so much nerve. Why, he used to astonish me with his jokes, even while he was suffering horribly. Suffer? I should say he did. The first week or ten days it was his feet. He kept saying, 'Oh, my God! my feet feel as though there were millions of needles being run through them.' I

used to squeeze his feet and toes in both my
hands, as hard as I possibly could, and that
seemed the only relief he could get. The day
he was shot and on Sunday he kept talking
all the time, but Monday he let up some, and
then Tuesday morning the doctors shut down
on his talking. Sunday morning, just after
the big crowd had cleared away, I was alone
with the General and Dr. Bliss. The Doctor
sat on one side of the bed and I on the other.
General Garfield had hold of Dr. Bliss's hand,
and turned his head and asked me if I knew
where he first saw Bliss. I told him I didn't,
and he then said he would tell me. He said
that when he was a youngster, and started for
the college at Hiram, he had just fifteen dollars—a ten dollar bill in an old leather pocketbook, which was in the breast-pocket of his
coat, and the other, five, was in his trousers
pocket. He said he was footing it up the
road, and as the day was hot, he took off his
coat and carried it on his arm, taking good
care to feel every moment or two for the
pocketbook, for the hard-earned fifteen dollars
was to pay his entrance at the college. After
awhile he got to thinking over what college
life would be like, and forgot all about the

pocketbook for some time, and when he went to look for it, it was gone.

"He went back mournfully along the road, hunting on both sides for the pocketbook. After awhile he came to a house where a young man was leaning over a gate, and who asked him as he came up what he was hunting for. Garfield explained his loss, and described the property, when the young man handed it over. The President by this time was laughing, and concluded, 'That young man was Bliss, wasn't it, Doctor?' The Doctor laughed and said yes, and when General Garfield said 'he saved me for college,' answered, 'Yes, and maybe if I hadn't found your ten dollars you wouldn't have been President of the United States.' The President laughed at that, and said that if he got well, and made any mistakes in his administration, Bliss would have to take the blame."

The Dead President

Dead! The President! Aye, and murdered,
    too!
The vilest deed that fiendish hate could do
Hath laid him low! The President is dead!
'A Nation, horror stricken, bows its head,

And, like to him, o'ercome by poignant grief,
Finds no expressions for the heart's relief.

Yes, he is dead! He, who to loftiest rise
Of Fame's high summit, toiled beneath the
    eyes
Of watching millions; whose success was won
By earnest, honest work—life's labor done—
Now lies enveloped in a sweet repose,
Though horrors dark presaged life's evening's
    close.

Words are but feeble things at best. They
    grow
Too weak to sound the lowest depths of woe,
E'en when a Nation mourns its heavy loss;
But when affection's gold is turned to dross,
Ah! then, what language can express the
    thought
Of them that suffer thus, what death hath
    wrought!

But yesterday, a man—now, lifeless clay!
But yesterday, the President! To-day
He fills a niche in Fame's historic hall,
And in those hearts that loved him. That
    is all!

'Tis all; but yet enough; for none are left
To hate. With one accord, like one bereft
Of near and dear ones, all the people bow
And bind the cypress on his stricken brow.

J. S. SLATER.

PRESIDENT ARTHUR

He Takes the Oath of Office

Sworn in as the Chief Executive officer of the Nation, at his residence in New York, by Chief Justice Brady. How he received the sad news.

By the Associated Press.

New York, Sept. 19.—In accordance with the dispatch received from the Cabinet in regard to taking the oath of office, messengers were sent to the different Judges of the Supreme Court. The first to put in an appearance was Judge John R. Brady, who was closely followed by Justice Donohue. The party, comprising the Vice-President and the judges named, besides District Attorney Rollins, and Elihu Root, and the eldest son of the new President, assembled in the front parlor of No. 123 Lexington Avenue (General Arthur's residence), where the oath of office was administered. The President has not signified his intentions as to when he would visit the Capital, and he declined to be interviewed as to his future course.

Special to *The Republican*.

New York, Sept. 20—12.30 a. m.—The first news of the President's death was announced at the theatres, the managers announcing briefly the sad event, and dropping the curtain upon the closing scenes of the performances at the various theatres. The news was received here without special excitement on the street, though at the Fifth Avenue Hotel, and other places of resort of prominent politicians, stock operators, etc., there was much comment as to the incidents of the late President's illness and the possible change of the policy and personnel of the incoming administration. Such comment was expressive strongly of sympathy with the late President, and confidence in President Arthur. It is authoritatively asserted that President Arthur will leave New York early this morning for Washington, and will reach the National Capital during the day, where he will take the oath of office as President. A train over the Pennsylvania road has been at his disposal for several days past, in anticipation of the death of General Garfield. The announcement has not been received here as yet regarding funeral arrangements. At half-past twelve o'clock, it is reported that General Arthur will join the Cabinet of the late President, at Long Branch, at once.

THE CAPITOL DRAPED IN MOURNING

Long Branch, N. J., Sept. 20.—Sergeant-at-arms Thompson, who is here, has telegraphed to drape the Capitol in mourning and have a catafalque built upon which to place the remains. The body will leave here some time to-morrow morning. The hour will be known definitely after the consultation with respect to an inquest, and the New Jersey law applicable thereto. This consultation is now being held between the United States Attorney for this district and the attorney for Monmouth county.

CHAPTER VI

UNDER PRESIDENT ARTHUR

After the death of Garfield, when Mr. Arthur became President of the United States, he didn't move into the White House right away, but occupied the granite building which belonged to Benjamin F. Butler, on the south side of the Capitol. He transacted all his business there, and it was his home for a certain length of time, until the White House could be put in order.

One morning a man came to the White House before the President had moved into it and said to me, "I would like to see the President." I replied, "The President is not here. He is in the Butler house, on the south side of the Capitol, but I do not believe that you will be able to see him." The man seemed to be perfectly rational, and talked in a sensible manner. About two weeks after the same man made his appearance at the White House again, and took a seat in the main vestibule.

My fellow-usher, Mr. Allen, went up to him, and asked him what he wanted. He said he wanted to see the President, and took a note out of his side-pocket and handed it to Mr. Allen. Mr. Allen read the note and brought it over to me, where I was standing at the foot of the main stairway. He said after he had read the note, "Tom, that man is crazy." I said, "We had better try and keep him here until Sergeant Dinsmore comes." After awhile Sergeant Dinsmore came in, and we stated the case to him. He went over to the man and said, "Come with me and I will get you to see the President." The man evidently mistrusted something, and made a bolt for the front door. Dinsmore grabbed him by the collar, and as he did so, the man's hand went down into his hip-pocket. With that I rushed up, and we clinched the man, and we downed him right inside of the door. While Mr. Dinsmore held his head down, Allen went for his hip-pocket and drew out a revolver, a six-shooter, with every barrel loaded. I took possession of that, and Dinsmore lifted him upon his feet. He was a muscular man, and a very ugly customer to handle. After they got down to police headquarters, inquiry was made as to what part of the country he came from. He was a prominent physician from the State of Pennsylvania, and he was sent to his home by the Police Department, and that was the last we ever saw of him.

One day, before the President had moved up to the White House, he came with Mrs. Judge Davis to see what was necessary to be done before he moved in. Mrs. Judge Davis looked through the glass of the door, and called me from the inner corridor. She said to me, as we were standing in front of the Blue Parlor, the President standing by, "How long has it been since this hall was decorated?" I said, "Not since Andrew Johnson was President." That settled the question. A few days after that the President had an interview with Colonel Rockwell, Commissioner of Public Buildings and Grounds, and said to him, "Colonel Rockwell, I want thus and so done, and thus and so done." The Colonel said, "Mr. President, there is no money to do it with." The President said, "You go ahead and do the work. I will not live in a house looking this way. If Congress does not make an appropriation, I will go ahead and have it done, and pay for it out of my own pocket.

I will not live in a house like this." Everything was done in accordance with his wish, and Congress made the appropriation to pay for it.

After everything had been put in proper order the President moved in. Mrs. McElroy, the President's sister, did the honors of the White House. Her drawing-room receptions were very fine. Mr. MacMichaels, of Philadelphia, was the Marshal of the District at the time. He generally made the presentations to Mrs. McElroy. They would usually have three relays of young ladies. One relay would take part in receiving for a certain length of time, then another relay would take their places, and they would form the background, back of the line. Mrs. McElroy was a very pleasant lady, and did the honors of the White House splendidly.

A sad event occurred in the beginning of Arthur's administration. Mr. Allen, dean of the Diplomatic Corps from the Hawaiian Islands, was in the Blue Parlor, close by where I was standing on duty. The diplomats had all been received, and the Judges of the Supreme Court had also been received. The diplomats and their ladies had left in order to hold their

own receptions. I noticed that Mr. Allen
pulled out his gold watch, which was a very
handsome one, to see what time it was, then
left the Blue Parlor to get his wraps at the
little room on the right-hand side of the vestibule, at the main door. Jerry Smith was
about to hand him his wraps. He stood at the
end of the sofa, and was trembling violently,
and in five minutes he fell dead. Word was
conveyed to the President, and the whole reception was stopped immediately. He was
put into a carriage and carried to his home.
There was a gloom cast over the White House
for that entire day, for it was the first New
Year's reception that was held after the death
of poor Garfield. The dinner parties and receptions held during Arthur's administration
were very fine. The President was very
gentlemanly in his manner. I recollect that
upon one occasion as I was going into the
Green Room with some ladies, showing them
through, I unexpectedly met the President
coming from the Blue Parlor with some ladies,
and in an instant he said to the ladies and myself, "I beg pardon." The President with his
ladies passed on into the Green Room, and

127

I passed into the Blue Parlor with the ladies I was showing through.

One Saturday night the President gave a dinner party. Quite a number of his acquaintances came down from New York City, and each one of the gentlemen brought a little oyster fork from New York with him, and they used these forks in eating their oysters that night. I think they were then presented to the President as souvenirs.

The President was accustomed to retire very late, and sometimes the day would be pretty well advanced before he would get his breakfast. He gave a great many swell dinner parties, and the guests used to enjoy themselves hugely. He generally attended the church right across from the White House, St. John's Episcopal Church. Often in good weather he would walk over and walk back; if it were disagreeable, he would have the carriage ordered and go over in that. He was a thorough society President. Sometimes his friends would come from New York City and he would take great pleasure in showing them around. On one occasion Mrs. William Astor, of New York, with some friends, called on the President, and were escorted through the house by himself, an honor which pleased them greatly.

One of his personal friends was Mr. Tiffany, the New York jeweler, who would come and stay a week with him as one of his guests.

CHAPTER VII

UNDER PRESIDENT CLEVELAND

At the close of Arthur's administration, on the evening of the third of March, the President-elect, Mr. Cleveland, came over to the White House, and the President showed him all through and explained it to him. The next day, the fourth of March, after Cleveland had taken his seat, ex-President Arthur had a fine lunch prepared for the President and Vice-President, Mr. Hendricks, and I think a portion of his intended Cabinet. There were a great number of people calling who wanted to see the President—office hunters; the woods were full of them. A great many were permitted to go upstairs, with smiles on their faces. Quite a number of them would reappear with long faces, and filled with disappointment. There seemed to be no end to the office-sekers. A great many of them became tired out and went home, thoroughly discouraged. Miss Rose Cleveland, the President's

sister, did the honors of the White House up
to the time of his marriage, and probably remained there for a time afterwards. I must
say right here that I shall never forget Miss
Rose Cleveland's kindness to my dying
daughter. After she learned that she was sick,
she gave orders to have a box of beautiful cut
flowers sent to her each Saturday, up to a few
days before she died. I remember the
morning Miss Cleveland ordered the carriage to go to the depot to meet the intended bride, Miss Frances Folsom. It was
quite early in the morning when she started
down, found the train on time, and without
any delay brought the intended bride to the
Executive Mansion. I received a very pleasant smile and a bow from the intended bride
as I opened the White House door. The
house was put in order that day for the wedding in the evening. Just before the wedding,
Miss Cleveland came into the Blue Room and
requested me to light the candles in the two
large candlesticks at each side of the mantel.
They were married in the Blue Parlor, right
in front of the divan, facing north. I had the
pleasure of hearing all the ceremony, as I
stood just in the doorway between the Blue

and Red Parlors. The Reverend Dr. Sunderland, of the First Presbyterian Church, performed the wedding ceremony. They then went upstairs, donned their traveling suits, passed down the grand stairway, and out of the Blue Parlor door, into the south portico. As they passed out rice and slippers were thrown after them. They spent their honeymoon at Oakland, on the Baltimore and Ohio Railroad, above Cumberland. After their return the President settled down to business, and Mrs. Cleveland did the honors of the White House. Her drawing-room receptions were very popular, and she was a great favorite with all the ladies that called. After she had been married about eighteen months, one morning quite early she came down to take her carriage to meet some invited guests at the train. Before she passed out I said to her, "Mrs. Cleveland, I have never had the pleasure of shaking hands with you since you have been in the White House." She said, "Is that so?" and in an instant her hand was up and gave mine a hearty shake. Sometimes Mrs. Cleveland would have a gathering of perhaps fifty or sixty friends, and have a musicale; sometimes in the Blue Parlor and some-

133

times in the Green Parlor. She was a very charming lady, and did the honors of the White House admirably. At the close of their first term I had the pleasure of seeing her down into her carriage, holding an umbrella over her, for the rain was pouring down, and bidding her good-bye. I was sorry to see her go. Before she left the White House, she made me a present of her photograph, with her autograph attached to it. I have that at my home to-day.

CHAPTER VIII

Under President Harrison

When President Harrison's administration began the office-seekers crowded in as usual. There were numerous plums to be picked, and the longest pole knocked the plums. A great many came away disappointed, with long faces. Others went away happy, for they had gained the prizes. The routine of drawing-room receptions and soirées went right along during the administration, and everything passed off very pleasantly indeed. During their administration Mrs. Harrison became quite an artist. She took lessons in painting. She would go out into the conservatory, and spend a great deal of time in painting orchids on china. She became quite proficient, and did some beautiful work. During the Harrison administration Mrs. McKee gave a ball in the East Room for the young ladies and gentlemen of her acquaintance. The room was decorated very nicely, and it was a swell affair.

Everything passed off charmingly, and everybody, when the ball was over, seemed to be happy. That was the second and last ball that was ever given in the White House.

"Baby McKee" seemed to be one of the principal personages in the White House. On one occasion there was a grand musicale given in the East Room by the "Bell Ringers." They made beautiful music. The family all assembled and listened very attentively. "Baby McKee" was with the President, and he made up his mind he was too far away from the music, so he broke away from the President and started over nearer to where the music was, although the President tried hard to keep him back. Evidently young "Baby McKee" was boss, for it was illustrated on that particular occasion.

There were dinner parties and receptions, such as are customary at the White House, and going out dining, and so on. In the latter part of the administration Mrs. Harrison was taken quite sick. She was taken out of this city, and up into the mountains of New York State, but in the month of September they brought her home again, and she had wasted away very much. It was during this period that the Grand Army of the Republic assembled in this city for its annual anniversary. The President had given orders to let them pass all through the Parlors. They kept coming all day until midnight, and this continued until everybody had seen all through the House.

It was during this administration that Secretary Tracy's wife and daughter and the daughter's maid were burned to death. Mrs. Tracy jumped out of the third-story window to escape the fire, and was killed. Two minutes later they rescued Secretary Tracy. If they hadn't come upon the scene just when they did, he would have been dead, as he was unconscious when rescued. Their home was burned to ruins. The President gave orders to have Mrs. Tracy and Miss Tracy brought over to the White House, and their remains laid in state in the East Room, under the centre chandelier. The arrangements were made for the funeral to take place from the East Room and, in the meantime, the President had had the Secretary brought over to the Mansion. He had returned to consciousness, and he was given the best of medical attention by the skilled physicians of the Navy. Poor

Mr. Tracy came down to the funeral service. It was an exceedingly sad sight. When everything was ready to remove the remains from the White House, he was so completely crushed and overcome that the President had to take his arm and have him taken up to bed. During the Harrison administration Dr. Scott, the father of Mrs. Harrison, died in the White House, in the ninety-third year of his age. Mrs. Harrison continued sick; some days she would rally and feel a little better, but finally she grew worse again. About three o'clock in the morning, on one occasion while she was ill, she was suffering a great deal of pain in her side. Most of the servants had gone home, and all the rest of the help about the house was asleep, with the exception of her dressing-maid; she came to the head of the stairs and called for me and my partner to make a fire in the range as soon as we possibly could. We hurried back and cleaned out the range in the pantry and soon had a rousing fire going. In the meantime the maid had hurried down with flaxseed. We put it into the saucepan and soon had it boiling, and she hurried upstairs with a flaxseed poultice and applied it to Mrs. Harrison's

138

side, which gave her a good deal of relief. She lingered along for some time, and finally died in the Garfield Room, which is in the southwest corner of the White House. Her remains were brought down into the East Room, and laid under the centre chandelier.

William S. Parker was detailed at the Executive Mansion December 27, 1892, in the Harrison administration.

CHAPTER IX

Cleveland's Second Administration

The fourth of March on which Mr. Cleveland took the oath of office for the second time was one of the most blustering days imaginable. It was very cold and bleak. The first thing I did that night when I came on duty was to take a prescription out for one of the President's children, who was somewhat indisposed. Four years previous to that I had escorted Mrs. Cleveland to her carriage. It was pouring rain, and I had the pleasure of shaking hands with her and bidding her good-bye. Now I stood at the Blue Parlor door and let her in—the same door out of which she had gone four years before—and had a kindly handshake with her. She looked charming, and seemed to be perfectly happy.

The routine business went on as usual in the White House: dinner parties, receptions and so on. She made everybody who came there go away happy. She had a kindly way of making people feel at home. One morning Mrs. Cleveland had started to New York. That night after I had gone on duty, a little after midnight, the President rang his bell. I went upstairs into the library. I was on duty by myself, as my partner was taking his leave of absence. He said, "Pendel, here is a telegram I want you to take down to the Western Union, and have it sent to New York." He gave me the money to pay for it. I said, "Mr. President, I am by myself; how will I manage this?" I spoke up and said that perhaps Miss Lene, Mrs. Cleveland's dressing maid, would go down and tend to the door while I took the telegram. So the President said, "All right." When I got downstairs, I put the night latch on the door so that no one could get in during my absence unless she let them in. I returned and delivered the message to the President, gave him the change I had left after paying for the telegram, and returned to my duties.

One morning during his administration I was making the rounds before day, and when I came upstairs, there was a lady sitting on the sofa near the foot of the main stairway. She seemed to be almost out of breath. Mr.

Cleveland's Second Administration

Lewis, my partner, said to me, "I am going up to get a glass of water for this lady; be careful, keep your eye on her. She is crazy." He brought the glass of water. She drank it and thanked him very kindly. He went over to the other part of the hall and I got into conversation with her. After I had conversed a little while with her, she got out her pocketbook, took out a five dollar note and a two dollar note, and handing them to me said, "You take that and go and buy yourself some tobacco." I handed the money back to her, and kindly thanked her, and told her that I did not chew tobacco. She wore a sealskin sack, which evidently was very valuable. A beautiful cross was suspended from her neck, set with costly pearls. She seemed to be a devoted Catholic. Every now and then she would take the cross and kiss it. While in conversation with her I found out that she came from Boston. She gave me her address, No. 24 Upton Street, Boston. She gave me somewhat of the history of her life. She had married a wealthy Spaniard, but her husband was dead, and her little son was dead. She had a delusion that her husband's two brothers were seeking to take her life in order

143

to get the property away from her. It began
to get along then towards five o'clock, and
Mr. Lewis thought it was about time to get
her out of the house, and back to the hotel
where she was stopping. She told him she
was stopping at the Arlington. The hotel
clerk told Mr. Lewis that she rushed downstairs and out of the hotel very rapidly. The
night clerk sent one of the colored servants
after her, and she disappeared so rapidly that
the negro thought it was a ghost and came
back to the hotel without her. About two
weeks afterwards I was on duty at the front
door, and my partner was making the rounds
when the bell rang very violently, away before
daybreak. I opened the door and she sprang
in with an open letter in her hand, and said,
"I must see the President right away." I told
her it was entirely too early for the President
to see her, that she would have to come later
on. She was nearly out of breath when she
got inside the door. After I let her in, she
asked me if she couldn't sit down, so I directed
her to the same sofa on which she had sat two
weeks before. She asked me if she couldn't
lie down a little while. She did so and fell off
into a little doze for about fifteen minutes.

She seemed to be perfectly sane upon all other
subjects, except that of her husband and his
brothers. She was evidently a lady of refine-
ment, and had plenty of means, for she had
just previous to that received a remittance
from Boston of fifteen hundred louis. Mr.
Lewis said to me, "Now, Tom, I guess you
had better try and get her over to the hotel."
She took my arm, after we got outside of the
House, and we conversed on different subjects
until we crossed the avenue, when I said to
her, "Where are you stopping now?" By that
time we had got across to Riggs' Bank, and
she said she had been stopping at Welcker's,
a first-class hotel. I said, "We will go there."
She said, "No, I won't. Those negroes have
been walking up the hallways there with big
bulldog revolvers." I had my foot into it then.
I thought the thing over, and thought of the
Riggs House. I said to her, "Will you go to
the Riggs House?" She said she would, so
we proceeded to the Riggs House, stepped
up to the night clerk and she gave orders for
a single room very correctly. He called a
servant to show her up to her room; she
turned to me, shook hands with me and bid
me good-night, and thanked me very kindly.

After she had got out of hearing, I said to the night clerk, "She is crazy, and you will have to be very careful about her." He thanked me very kindly, I took my departure, and that was the last time I ever saw her, or heard of her.

Mrs. Cleveland was very popular during this administration. She held a great many receptions and they were immense affairs. After these receptions were over she would generally invite from fifty to one hundred people up in the grand corridor for tea. Some nights when she would come in from a dinner party I would be taking her up in the elevator, and she would remark to her lady friend, "I know it is twelve o'clock, for Mr. Pendel is on duty." They used to have quite a number of friends to come and spend a week. In carrying cards and notes into her dressing room, I always found it exceedingly pleasant. I recollect that on one occasion the President was called away suddenly to New York, shortly after their marriage, and left word that when I came on duty I should stay on my entire watch, and be close to Mrs. Cleveland's door. I did so, faithfully. She was very fond of canary birds and mocking birds. As I was

making my rounds on one occasion near her
room, her canary was near the window sill. A
great rat had forced his way into the cage, had
just killed the poor little canary and was going
to have a feast on him, when I arrived in time
to make for him. He burst through the door
and made his escape, and Mrs. Cleveland was
very sorry for it. I took the mocking bird
downstairs where I could have my eye on him
for fear the rat might return again. Afterwards Mrs. Cleveland had her pet canary
stuffed and put in her room.

Often they would give musicales in the Blue
Parlor of the White House. These were very
pleasant, and there would generally be from
thirty to forty guests to enjoy the music.
On one occasion, in conversation with one of
her friends, Mrs. Cleveland remarked, "Oh,
Mr. Pendel is one of the pillars of the White
House."

President Cleveland was a very plain, matter-of-fact man. On one occasion when I came
on duty at midnight, he was in the back end
of the upper corridor, trying to find a lamp,
I said, "Mr. President, is there anything I can
do for you?" And he said, "Yes, I am trying
to find a lamp." We both went back into the

library, and I arranged it for him on his desk, and he went on writing. He was a very hard worker—the hardest working President I ever saw in my life. I used to sit opposite the library door, so that I would be convenient to him whenever he wanted me, and always attended to his wants. It was sometimes three o'clock in the morning when he would retire. Between one and two o'clock one night he called me into his library and said, "Pendel, I wish you would take that mocking bird down. It annoys me." After I had removed him, the mocking bird got mad and would not sing a bit more. The President said to me, "Pendel, where did you put him?" "On Mr. Loeffler's desk," I said. He said, "You don't think he will catch cold there, do you?" I said, "Mr. President, I don't think he will, but, however, I will move him." I brought him into the inner corridor, and put him behind the screen where he was thoroughly protected. After the President had finished his work in the library, I said, "Mr. President, I have put him behind here, where he will not catch cold." He then said, "Oh, that is all right, Mr. Pendel."

Cleveland's Second Administration

It was during the first part of Mr. Cleveland's second administration that the Princess Eulalie, of Spain, and her husband visited this country; she was Spain's representative at the World's Fair. Upon arriving in this country she was chaperoned by one of our naval officers, Captain Davis. When she arrived at Washington she was met at the depot by the Secretary to the President, Mr. Henry T. Thurber, with the President's carriage, drawn by four horses, and escorted by a troop of cavalry from Fort Myer. It was Troop B, of the Fourth, the late General Lawton's troop.

The Princess was driven to the Arlington Hotel, where she remained while in the city. Soon after her arrival at the Arlington the Princess called at the Executive Mansion and paid her respects to the President and Mrs. Cleveland, who, later in the day, returned the Princess' visit.

The President gave a dinner in honor of the Princess, May 26, 1893. Upon the arrival of the guests, they were escorted to the library to lay aside their wraps, and then to the East Room to meet the President and Mrs. Cleveland. The Princess arrived a little late. Through the thoughtfulness of Mr. R. C.

Mitchell, one of the ushers, the Princess' wrap was taken in charge by him at the entrance to the Red Room, which saved her the trouble of going to the library. To the surprise of everybody the Princess walked directly into the East Room as if that were part of the programme. Some of the officials were awaiting her arrival on the second floor, from whence she was to be escorted to the East Room and presented to the President. These officials were very much surprised and chagrined when they learned that the Princess had gone to the East Room, unaccompanied except by her husband, and presented herself to the President and Mrs. Cleveland. The President noticed the Princess coming into the East Room, and, grasping the situation at a glance, very gracefully walked toward the Princess and received her with extended hand and a very gracious smile. Dinner was then served.

During the excitement caused by General Jacob S. Coxey, from Massillon, Ohio, with his so-called army, which camped at Brightwood Park, from April 26 to May 1, 1894, the guard at the White House was increased from twelve to twenty-six men, the Secretary to the President, Mr. Henry T. Thurber, having thought it advisable. It was then that I became acquainted with Mr. James Ciscle, one of the first of the reinforcements sent to the White House. After Coxey had abandoned his army, Mr. Thurber thought it advisable to still keep the full force owing to the unsettled condition of the times. Then came the Chicago railroad strike, and the calling out of Government troops, and the explosion of the caisson, killing forty-five men and wounding as many more. Lieutenant-General Schofield was then commanding the United States Army. President Cleveland, Secretary of War Daniel S. Lamont, Attorney-General Olney and General Schofield had consultations that lasted until long after midnight. The vestibule and corridors were thronged with newspaper men watching for the coming of some of the Cabinet. Sometimes they would wait for hours and then the Cabinet would have no news to give out. Meanwhile they would amuse themselves by telling funny stories and studying how they could get the news they wanted.

William McKinley

CHAPTER X

Under President McKinley

On the 3d of March the President-elect received an invitation from President Cleveland to dine with him, which he accepted. Owing to Mrs. McKinley's fatigue, due to much traveling, she did not attend the dinner. On March 4 the President-elect came to the White House and with President Cleveland rode to the Capitol in the same carriage, where he was inaugurated, and then returned to the White House. After the return there was a grand luncheon served and then the President reviewed the great procession. From that time and up until late in the night the social calling was immense. The next day was the same way. I was so busy that I could hardly manage all the people, showing them over the house, the private parlors and the bed chambers above.

After the return from the inauguration I met Mrs. McKinley, whom I had not seen for twenty years, in the Blue Parlor. She seemed to be very glad to see me and shook hands with me heartily.

For about ten days there was a continuous reception by the President of delegations, military companies, Governors of States with their staffs and their ladies, whom I showed all over the White House. More particularly I remember the Governor of Ohio. Sandwiched in between these delegations and military companies were prominent men of all nations. The White House at this time was the scene of many brilliant affairs.

From about the middle of March Mrs. McKinley would take daily drives, and always had to be assisted in going out or coming in. If the President was not with her, one of the ushers assisted her, bringing her down in the elevator. Often it would fall to my lot to assist her to her carriage.

Everything went on nicely and smoothly until just before Christmas of that year, when the President's mother was taken very ill. The family all went to Canton. The President and his wife watched by the bedside of his mother until she passed away. Of course this produced sadness in the White House, and all the receptions and dinner parties intended for that season were abandoned. For a long time afterward there was great grief and sorrow at the White House.

Following this sad bereavement and after the first shock had passed away, the season that followed was a very gay one, with dinner parties and levees up until the last public reception that was to have been given. Preparations were made and the House was being put in order to have the last public reception of that season, when on the morning of the 15th of February we received the terrible news of the blowing up of the "Maine" in the harbor of Havana. Two hundred and fifty-four of our brave sailors and marines, with two officers, were launched into eternity. It cast a gloom over our entire nation, and particularly the White House. The President immediately gave orders to discontinue the decorating, and that there should be no levee that night. Two months after war was declared against Spain. The order was given to raise many thousand troops, and from that time on for some months the tramp of regiments was heard and great numbers of soldiers were seen passing through the city of

Washington. There was great activity at the White House in the executive department, seeing military men and those applying for active positions in the Army and Navy. These were very stirring times. About this time Mr. Roosevelt came to the White House. He had just been appointed a colonel in the Rough Riders, and was accompanied by Col. John Jacob Astor, to whom he introduced me. I got both their autographs on that day, little thinking then that Mr. Roosevelt would be the next President of the United States.

The following season, while the war was going on, and things had settled down to a military routine the receptions were again taken up, and there were dinner parties, social gatherings and public receptions, and during that period, I think, there were two dancing parties given in the state dining-room, something that I had never seen given in that room before. Late that season the President took a trip to Lake Champlain with Mrs. McKinley, and it seemed to be very beneficial to both of them. They were gone about a month.

At the beginning of the next season a New Year's reception was held. After that the President was taken sick with the grip, and consequently all the receptions and dinner parties were over for that season. During this season the Postal Congress of the World met in Washington, and the President gave them a reception, which was well attended, notable people of all nations having gathered in the city. Just in the midst of it Mr. Preston, one of the representatives from the Hawaiian Islands to the Postal Congress, fell in the Green Parlor, dangerously ill. Mr. Ciscle sent for General Wood, who was then a surgeon in the Army, and with his assistance Mr. Preston revived enough to be taken to his hotel, where he died ten days afterwards.

An incident which came under my notice very lately is timely to mention here: Mr. Dawes, the Comptroller of the Currency, visited the White House with the Adjutant-General of the State of Illinois. After these gentlemen had gone upstairs, he said, as they came down to leave the house, "Mr. Pendel, come over, please, and we will take a seat in the East Room, for I want you to talk some to us." I sat down and had quite a chat with them, detailing much of my experience in the White House, and they both became very much interested in what I had to say. When

157

I arose to leave, the Adjutant-General said to me, "Have you a picture of yourself that you could let me have, and a written statement about the facts you have been telling us just now?" I told him that I had both things he wanted, and would hand them to Mr. Dawes, who could forward them to Illinois. He said to me before he left, "Your picture and this written statement shall have a prominent place in the Memorial Hall in the Lincoln Monument. They shall certainly be framed and placed there."

About this time some of the troops began to return. One of the first battalions that arrived was a battalion of marines, about five or six hundred strong. The President gave particular orders that when they returned to Washington he would be happy to have them pass in review at the White House. I recall that it was a very rainy afternoon when they arrived and there was a great multitude of people to see them as they passed in review through the portico, where the President and his Cabinet reviewed them, and they shared together the heartiest congratulations and cheers of the people.

Under President McKinley

Then came the campaign for McKinley's re-
election. There was a great deal of excitement among the politicians, both parties being
sanguine that their candidate would be
elected. But President McKinley was re-
elected by an overwhelming majority.

During Mr. McKinley's first administration
John Addison Porter, his private secretary,
passed away. Also the Vice-President, Garrett A. Hobart, who was a fine man and an
elegant gentleman. I remember presenting
him with one of my autographs, for which he
thanked me very kindly. Of course, the death
of our Vice-President brought sadness to the
Administration, for he was a man very much
beloved.

The day of his second inauguration was a
very wet, dismal one. Nevertheless, there
was a great multitude of people in the city to
view the procession, which was a most remarkable one. After the procession a grand
luncheon was given. There were present Mr.
and Mrs. Abner McKinley, Miss Helen Gould,
Mrs. Sartoris, Mrs. Gen. Fred Grant, and
quite a number of the notable people of
our nation. The procession lasted until
almost dark, but the President stayed faith-

fully in the reviewing stand until they had all passed. After the procession he received people until about 9 o'clock, when with the guests of the house, he and Mrs. Mc-Kinley attended the Inaugural Ball, which was a grand affair given in the Pension Office. The following day a great many persons called. Military companies, Governors of States, clubs and bands of music were admitted into the East Room as they marched up in lines, the music enlivening everything about the White House. The President and Mrs. McKinley seemed to be perfectly happy and pleased to see the great multitudes that were calling on them. The President always took great delight in shaking hands with the people. He told one of the officials at the White House that he took more delight in shaking hands with the people than he did at one of the state dinners. It seemed to be a great gratification to him to meet the masses of the people.

Mrs. McKinley was remarkably fond of little children. Sometimes on going out to take her drive and little children being near, she would throw them a kiss if they were not near enough to the carriage for her to kiss them. The President was very kind and gentle to her at all times. Often I would go in with cards after she had recovered from spells of sickness after dinner. They would be sitting in the grand corridor near the entrance to the dining-room. She would have her knitting, which she was very fond of, and the President would be reading his paper or looking over some documents that required his attention. He seemed to do everything in his power to please her. They were a very happy man and wife.

On Saturday evenings during his administration there would often be gatherings of a few friends in the Blue Parlor after dinner, and hymn books would be brought out and then all would join in singing hymns, accompanied by the piano. Frequently when the President returned from church on the Sabbath he would hum the tune of a hymn as I was taking him up in the elevator. On one occasion there was a lady guest at the White House who accompanied the President to church. When they returned, on seeing me, he said to her, "This man has been here about thirty-five years." There were two busts near the Red Parlor and he asked whose busts they were. I answered, "Mr. President, one of them is John Bright, the English statesman, and the other is John Jay, Chief Justice of the United States. The President was very fond of music and singing, as was also Mrs. McKinley. Her taste was beautiful in the way of decorative work.

Last season the social functions were discontinued at the White House on account of the illness of Mrs. McKinley, who was so feeble that we used to have a rolling chair for her, in which we took her up and down stairs bodily. Finally she rallied enough and improved so nicely that they made a trip to Canton and then they took the long trip to California. While she was there she was at the very point of death. I never expected to see her return alive to the White House. The San Francisco trip was looked forward to with a great deal of pleasure. All arrangements for the trip went on harmoniously and nicely. Trains were fitted up and those connected with the Pennsylvania Railroad took the greatest care in endeavoring to make everything as happy as they possibly could for Mr. and Mrs. McKinley. Mr. Stone, who is now an usher at the White House, but formerly a conductor of the Pullman Palace Car Company, accompanied them on this trip. Before they arrived at San Francisco, Mrs. McKinley began to show signs of failing health. By the time San Francisco was reached, she was desperately ill, and the very best medical skill was obtained for her. But she recovered, and was enabled to take the homeward trip, which was a perfect miracle, considering the fact that her life seemed to just hang on a thread while there. They returned to the White House, where she was still under the care of physicians. Finally she was able to take her carriage drives again.

On the 5th of July last they started for Canton to spend probably most of the summer there. They then went to Buffalo to visit the Exposition which was being held there.

On the 6th of September, about twenty-five minutes past four in the afternoon, Jerry Smith, one of the servants at the White House, came to the foot of the stairs and called up to me, "The President is shot!" He had been cleaning in the telegraph room and had heard the awful news. Scarcely believing my ears, I called out, "What, Jerry?" He said again, "The President has been shot!" I

did not think it could be so, supposing it was
some wild rumor that had gotten out. I asked
Mr. Gilbert, one of the specially appointed
policemen on duty at the White House,
to try and find out if the news was true, but
they were so busy in the telegraph room that
we could not hear anything. Mr. Gilbert was
skeptical, as well as myself, as to whether the
report was true. About twenty minutes after
this a newspaper man came hurrying to the
White House with the news. Then there was
a sad gloom all over the house. Men were
coming to and fro, asking questions continu-
ally. We continued to receive word from
Buffalo of the President's condition, and were
very much encouraged from the favorable
tone of most of them. On the 12th of September we were particularly glad, as on that
morning he partook of a cup of coffee, a piece
of toast and a soft-boiled egg, and we all
thought that in about two weeks he would
be able to return to the White House. On
that night there was a turn for the worse. His
physicians were called in and worked hard
over him, but with the sad result that we all
know so well. On Friday he grew worse and
worse. I remained at the White House that

night until ten o'clock. The news continued
to come in worse and gloom and sadness fell
over the whole city and over the nation. Saturday morning, the 14th of September, at
twenty-five minutes after two o'clock, he
passed away. And there was sorrow and
weeping all over our land. My little home
was among the very first to be draped in
mourning.

He laid in state Sunday and part of Monday at Buffalo. Tuesday night the remains
were brought to Washington. Mrs. McKinley, with Dr. Rixey and Mr. Abner McKinley,
came to the White House probably half an
hour before the remains arrived. It was a
very sad sight. Previous to his remains being brought in the undertaker came and was
making arrangements for the casket to be
laid under the centre chandelier in the East
Room. He was just arranging so as to have
his head lay to the south and his feet to the
north. Seeing this, I told him that President
Lincoln's remains laid with the head to the
north and his feet to the south. The undertaker immediately changed the position so
that he laid as Mr. Lincoln did. After the remains had been brought in and the two sol-

diers and two marines had taken their position at the head and foot of the casket, Mrs. McKinley came in on the arm of Dr. Rixey to take a long look at her dear husband. It was very sad. Again in the morning she took her final farewell of the remains before they were removed to the Capitol. I have at my home, pressed and carefully preserved, one of the leaves from the many flowers which kept arriving all the time.

President McKinley was a remarkable man; he was genial, a natural magnet. He drew the masses of the people to him. Always had a kind word, greeting with the extension of his hand every one that called on him, and endeavored to make them feel happy and at home.

As the funeral train passed through the towns on its way to Washington and Canton, great crowds met and sang in concert his favorite hymn, "Lead, Kindly Light," and the hymn containing his last words, "Nearer, My God, to Thee."

After the funeral at Canton, President Roosevelt returned to Washington and took up his residence at his sister's, Mrs. Cowles, on N Street. In a few days he came to the

White House to reside, and shortly after his family arrived from Oyster Bay.

Then the people began to recover from the sad events that had transpired and began to call on President Roosevelt. He has been a very busy man ever since he entered upon his duties. I would term him a great President and his wife a great lady, perfectly plain, matter-of-fact persons. Both he and she always have a kind salutation for those who are connected with the White House, from the very humblest to those holding high position. There has hardly been a day since he has settled down at the White House but that he has had some friends to luncheon with him, and quite a number of private dinners. He seems to be very popular. I am satisfied that he is going to make us a splendid President.

In conclusion, I must say that I hope I shall never live to see again what I have seen during the last thirty-seven years in the White House, as I have been on duty there when the three great tragedies of our country were enacted. There is no other man in the nation to-day who can say this. There is no living soul connected with the White House outside of myself who was there on the first day I entered on duty, the 3d of November, 1864, when the great rebellion was raging and when there was weeping and mourning all over our land for those who had fallen in the ranks on both sides of that great conflict.

CHAPTER XI

List of Furniture and Bric-a-brac in Executive Mansion, compiled from data furnished by Mr. Pendel, Usher, by direction of Col. F. A. Bingham, April 5, 1898.

MAIN VESTIBULE

The three large Gothic chairs and the two marble mantels have been there since the days of Abraham Lincoln.

The tiling of the floors was done under Hayes' administration.

EAST ROOM

An old-fashioned chandelier hung where the present centre chandelier now hangs; under that chandelier the remains of Abraham Lincoln lay in state.

The present chandeliers were put in during General Grant's second administration; were made in Germany, and cost $1800 each. Each chandelier contains 5060 pieces of cut glass.

Under the centre chandelier the following distinguished persons lay in state after their death:

Mrs. Harrison, wife of President Harrison.

Wife and daughter of Gen. B. F. Tracy, Secretary of the Navy during Harrison's administration.

Doctor Scott, Mrs. Harrison's father, who was ninety-three years of age.

W. Q. Gresham, Secretary of State under President Cleveland.

The electric globes in the ceiling were put in during Harrison's administration.

I was showing Mrs. Lee, wife of Admiral Lee (now nearly 90 years of age), through the White House in Arthur's administration. She told me that Dolly Madison told her that she had that painting of Washington cut out of its frame in 1814, for safe keeping when the English burnt the Capitol and a portion of the interior of the White House.

The painting of Lincoln by Coggswell was purchased in Grant's second term; cost, $2500.

The painting of Martha Washington is by E. F. Andrews.

The painting of Jefferson is by E. F. Andrews.

The painting of Washington is by an English artist, name not now remembered, previous to the War of 1812. When the artist finished the work he wanted his money (only $800) and the Government was not able to pay him. A citizen advanced the money for the Government, and paid him.

Green Room

The large cabinet in this room was selected by President Arthur.

The large pair of Chinese vases (about four feet high), standing on the hearth, were also selected by President Arthur.

The clock on the mantel was selected by Mrs. Grant when in the White House.

The brass statuette on the pier table was selected by Mrs. Grant. It is said to be a copy of one taken from the ruins of Pompeii.

The Japanese punch bowl on the cabinet has been there since the days of Abraham Lincoln.

The small cabinet in this room was selected by President Arthur.

171

Blue Parlor

The clock on the mantel is said to be a present from the first Napoleon to Lafayette, and from Lafayette to our Government.

Standing near the hearth on the east side of this room, is a pair of candle stands, probably five feet high. While showing an old, gray-haired gentleman through the White House in Arthur's administration, he told me that they were a present from General Patterson, of Philadelphia (now dead and gone), to General Jackson, when he was President of the United States.

The pair of vases on the pier table on the west side of the room were a present from the French Government to ours. They are the Sèvres ware. On one of them is a picture of Charlotte Corday, who assassinated Marat in his bath in 1792 or 1793. She was beheaded for it. On the other is a picture of Marie Antoinette, who was also beheaded during the French Revolution.

The framework of the furniture, the pier table and the marble mantel have all been in this room since the days of Abraham Lincoln.

The door opening out on to the south portico is the one they brought poor Garfield through the day he was shot, to avoid the multitude of people that had gathered at the north front.

The tiling on the south portico was put down in Harrison's administration.

Red Parlor

The antique cabinet mantel, the two cabinets, bookcase and centre table, all made by Louis Tiffany, the artist, of New York, were purchased by direction of President Arthur.

The tapestry fire screen was a present from the Austrian Government; the presentation was made by the Austrian Minister about two months before General Grant's second term expired.

The French clock has been there since the days of Abraham Lincoln.

The vase on the small table, representing a cactus in bloom, was selected by President Arthur.

The brown pitcher and bowl standing on one of the cabinets on the west side of the room, came from the Birmingham establishment in England, and were selected by Mrs. Grant.

The two bronze figures on the same cabinet, and the two on the next cabinet, were selected by Mrs. Grant.

STATE DINING ROOM

The brass pheasant, with her brood of little ones, standing on one of the side tables, fronting to the south, was selected by Mrs. Grant.

The four candelabras, which are used sometimes for decorating the state dining table, were selected by Mrs. Hayes.

The five fruit stands are very old, and more than likely have been there since the days of Thomas Jefferson.

The set of chairs with oval backs have been there since the days of Abraham Lincoln.

The set of chairs with straight pieces in the back were made in New York City, and were selected by President Arthur.

The sideboard and sidetable have also been there since the days of Abraham Lincoln, and perhaps a long time before.

The plateau is sometimes used on the state dining table to represent a lake of water.

Furniture in Executive Mansion

It is very old, and probably has been there since the days of Thomas Jefferson.

The white marble mantels are of colonial style, and have been there probably since the house was built.

During the Hayes administration, two glass doors were cut through so as to open into the conservatory from the west end.

PRIVATE DINING ROOM

The buffet, on the west side of the room, was carved in Cincinnati, Ohio, and purchased during Hayes' administration.

The two sidetables are very old; have been there since the days of Abraham Lincoln, and before.

The silver ship, which has been used on the state dining table, was selected by Mrs. Grant at the Centennial in Philadelphia, for the Government. It represents the "Ship of State," and contains the inscription,

> "All alone went Hiawatha
> Through the clear, transparent water,"

taken from Longfellow's poem, "Hiawatha." Made by the Gorham Silver Company.

175

CORRIDOR

The two chairs, made of elks' horns, were selected by President Arthur.

The white marble table near the stairway, was formerly used as a centre table in the Red Room, when Abraham Lincoln was in the White House.

The two white marble pier tables, in west end of corridor, south side, set partly into the wall, used to stand between the Green and Red Rooms, main corridor, and were removed to their present position during Grant's administration.

The grand stairway at west end of corridor was put up in Grant's administration, by General Babcock, an engineer officer in the army.

The mosaic screen was put in during Arthur's administration by Louis Tiffany, the artist, of New York City.

The furniture (sofas and chairs) were selected by Mrs. Cleveland.

There is a pair of delicate, blue vases in one of the private chambers upstairs, which were selected by Mrs. Grant. They are from the city of Venice. On the lid of each vase is the head of an Egyptian boar.

176